Effective Discipline
in Primary Schools
and Classrooms

The Authors

Pamela Munn worked as a secondary school teacher in London before becoming a research fellow in the Education Department of Stirling University. She was involved in research on accountability in education and latterly on curriculum innovation before taking up post as lecturer in applied research in education at York University where she was involved in helping teachers research their own schools and classrooms. Since 1986 she has been Depute Director of the Scottish Council for Research in Education. Her work there has included research on adult education, school boards and teacher recruitment.

Margaret Johnstone has been involved in educational research for sixteen years, working on a wide range of topics. Since 1986 she has been a researcher at the Scottish Council for Research in Education. Her work there has included a study of stress in teaching, a survey of truancy in secondary schools and the production of a package for teachers giving information on action against bullying.

Valerie Chalmers worked as a primary school teacher in a range of different schools before becoming involved in research into the training of primary school teachers. From that she moved on to join the research team investigating discipline in schools. She has now taken up a post in the Primary Development Department at Northern College of Education.

EFFECTIVE DISCIPLINE IN PRIMARY SCHOOLS AND CLASSROOMS

PAMELA MUNN
MARGARET JOHNSTONE
and
VALERIE CHALMERS

P·C·P
Paul Chapman
Publishing Ltd

Paul Chapman Publishing Ltd
144 Liverpool Road
London
N1 1LA

British Library Cataloguing in Publication Data
Munn, Pamela
   Effective discipline in primary schools and classrooms.
   I. Title II. Johnstone, Margaret, *1941*– III. Chalmers, Valerie
   372.11024

ISBN 1 85396 174 4

Typeset by Inforum Typesetting, Portsmouth
Printed and bound by Athenaeum Press Ltd,
Newcastle upon Tyne.

CONTENTS

Acknowledgements viii
Preface ix

1 EFFECTIVE DISCIPLINE 1
 The structure of the book 2
 What is effective discipline? 3
 Do schools make a difference? 6
 The schools 6
 How was information about the schools' discipline
 policy and practice collected? 11
 What can we learn from the intensive study of four schools? 11
 References 16

2 THE SCHOOL'S VIEWS OF ITS PUPILS 17
 How did the schools view their pupils? 18
 School differences in effective discipline: an overview 23
 Teacher–pupil relationships 24
 Rules 26
 Sanctions 28
  The verbal rebuke 28
  Punishment exercises 30
 Rewards and praise 31
 Are pupils aware of their school's views? 33
 Conclusion 35
 Investigating your own school's view of its pupils 39
 References 39

3 STAFF RELATIONSHIPS AND DISCIPLINE   41
   The role of the headteacher and management team   42
   Differences among the schools   45
      The role of the AHT   45
      Restricted freedom as support   46
      Whose pupil is it?   49
   Teacher–teacher relationships   51
   Conclusion   54
   Reviewing staff relationships in your school   55
      For unpromoted staff   55
      For promoted staff   56
   References   56

4 A FRAMEWORK FOR UNDERSTANDING CLASSROOM
   DISCIPLINE   57
   Choosing the teachers   58
   How did we collect information about teachers' classroom practice? 58
   Making sense of effective classroom discipline   59
   The importance of planning   60
   Reacting to disruption   62
   Influences on teachers' actions   62
      Conditions   62
      Goals   64
   The interplay of goals, conditions and actions   66
   How do teachers know how to promote good behaviour?   68
   How can experienced teachers help new teachers?   69
      Helping beginning teachers to analyse classroom practice 70
      Helping beginning teachers to reflect upon their practice 71
      Helping beginning teachers to develop their lesson planning 71
   References   72

5 PROMOTING EFFECTIVE CLASSROOM DISCIPLINE   74
   What do teachers do to get their classes to work well?   74
   Conditions   79
   Goals   83
   Do goals and conditions predict actions?   86
   Summary   87
   References   88

6 PUPILS' VIEWS ON DISCIPLINE   89
   Classroom discipline   89
   What do teachers do to get the class to work well?   90
   Are there patterns in pupil perceptions?   93
   Classroom discipline and school discipline   96
      The 'school' perception of teacher actions   96

Classroom rules and sanctions 97
School rules and sanctions 99
A pupil is a pupil 100
How did pupils see rule-breaking and its resolution? 101
Means and ends – why is discipline needed? 102
Conclusion 102
References 103

7 PARENTS AND EFFECTIVE DISCIPLINE 104
Who decides what counts as good discipline: teachers or parents? 105
Are parents really welcome? Different approaches to parental
  involvement in discipline 108
Conclusion 117
Assessing parental involvement in your school 120
References 120

8 WHAT CAN SCHOOLS DO TO IMPROVE DISCIPLINE? 122
A checklist for examining school discipline 124
  Expectations of pupils 124
  Expectations of teachers 124
  Expectations of parents 125
  Expectations about senior management: practical activities
    for senior staff 125
Classroom discipline 127
Links between whole school and classroom practice 128
References 130

RESEARCH APPENDIX: Research Design, Data Collection
  and Analysis 131
The rationale for a case-study approach 132
Whole school discipline 133
  Data collection and analysis: from teachers 133
  Data collection and analysis: from pupils 133
  Data collection and analysis: from documents 134
  Data collection and analysis: from field notes 135
Classroom discipline 135
  Data analysis 136
Conclusion 137

References 138

Index 139

ACKNOWLEDGEMENTS

This research was funded by the Scottish Office Education Department (SOED) whose support and encouragement is gratefully acknowledged. The research would not have been possible without the help and co-operation of the teachers and pupils in the case-study schools who spared time to be interviewed and who discussed our findings. Our particular thanks go to the teachers whose classroom practice we studied. Our project advisory committee offered us constructive criticism and encouragement, and Janette Finlay typed successive drafts quickly and accurately.

The views and interpretations reported are those of the authors and are not necessarily those of SOED or the Scottish Council for Research in Education.

We are grateful to Sally Brown and Donald McIntyre for their permission to reproduce their work on teachers' goals and on procedures for analysing data on teachers' professional craft knowledge.

PREFACE

This book has grown out of a research study commissioned by the Scottish Office Education Department (SOED). The three-year study investigated discipline in secondary and primary schools. Its focus was on understanding the policy and practice of a small number of schools. It set out to explore what these policies were and what had influenced them. It also studied experienced teachers in action in the classroom in an attempt to understand what they did to get their classes to work well.

The book and its companion volume, *Effective Discipline in Secondary Schools and Classrooms*, offer teachers, teacher educators and advisers a framework for explaining why schools adopt particular approaches to discipline. They suggest a number of activities which schools could undertake to review their own practice and describe the benefits and costs of the policies in the research schools. At classroom level, they describe experienced teachers' practice, offer a framework for understanding that practice and suggest ways in which it could be used in pre-service and in-service training.

Discipline is a topic which has generated an extensive literature, ranging from small-scale sociological studies of individual schools and classrooms, and psychological studies using experimental and control groups, to the number-crunching approaches of large surveys of discipline. There have been more studies of indiscipline than of good discipline, as previous reviews of the literature have pointed out. Our research has concentrated on discipline, not indiscipline, and on what teachers and pupils see as contributing to good discipline. There are some surprising omissions in the views we report. For example, there are few references to the curriculum as a factor promoting good discipline, perhaps because the common curriculum, mixed ability teaching and public examinations for all are now taken for granted. Similarly, there are few references to timetabling, physical features of the school, school size or links with social welfare agencies. Our open approach to collecting information and our emphasis on discipline rather than indiscipline may have led teachers to concentrate on matters of most immediate direct practical concern to them, such as the nature of their pupil population, rather than on espoused theories. We cannot, of course, claim that the frameworks we offer are comprehensive or complete, only that they are starting points for schools and teachers wanting to review their own practice. The book ends with a checklist of activities schools can undertake to explore their own practice. It argues that real and lasting improvements to discipline can be made only by understanding the influences on their current practice. We hope that teachers will be encouraged to look afresh at what they do and use the book as a springboard for ideas about developing and improving their school and class-room discipline.

1
EFFECTIVE DISCIPLINE

As every teacher knows, there is no infallible recipe for ensuring effective discipline. Instead, each school and teacher adopt a range of strategies which seem appropriate to their own particular circumstances and which are more or less effective. Teachers get few opportunities to hear about what happens outside their own classroom or school and, when they do, the emphasis is on problem schools and pupils, not on success. Indiscipline, not good discipline, is what makes headlines and much of the writing on discipline concentrates on the causes of, and cures for, bad behaviour. It is relatively unusual for teachers to hear about what their colleagues are doing well and to learn about what encourages good practice.

This book describes how schools promote and maintain effective discipline at two levels:

- whole school policy and practice;
- classroom policy and practice.

It sets out what schools count as effective discipline and the influences on these definitions. Its aim is to help teachers and others analyse their own approaches to discipline by presenting information about the rather different approaches used in four primary schools, and explaining why things were the way they were in these schools. Each school's approach to discipline was seen as effective by staff and pupils, but it is not our intention that others should mimic their practice. Schools wanting to improve their discipline need to begin by understanding why their current practice is the way it is. Only then can they plan real and lasting improvements. This book provides a starting point for schools wanting to analyse their discipline policy and practice. It demonstrates that there were three key influences on discipline in the schools studied. These were:

- the school's view of its pupils;
- staff relationships and the special role of the headteacher;
- the extent and quality of parental involvement.

Examples are provided of how these factors influenced discipline, and ways in which teachers can detect the influence of these factors in their own schools are suggested. The book also describes the rules, sanctions and rewards systems in operation in the four schools, and the part played by the headteacher and other senior staff in promoting discipline. As in all human affairs, there are costs and benefits to any course of action. These are pointed out as we go along and summarised at the end of each chapter. The approaches taken by the different schools offer ideas for teachers to debate and discuss.

At classroom level, the book examines what different teachers do to promote effective discipline and uses the similarities among the teachers' practice to construct a framework describing:

- the different actions teachers take, with emphasis on the importance of advance preparation and planning;
- the importance of the classroom context, particularly the teachers' beliefs about their pupils;
- the influence of goals on teachers' actions.

Again, we are not suggesting that teachers mimic the actions described by the experienced teachers in the research project. Instead, we suggest that those wanting to think about and analyse their own classroom practice use the framework as a guide. We see the framework as being particularly useful to teacher educators and beginning teachers. Our belief is that only by teachers understanding what they do and why they do it will they have a sure basis for development and improvement.

The structure of the book

Chapters 2 to 3 discuss the key influences on the schools' definition of effective discipline and on the operation of discipline policy, and illustrate the rather different approaches used. There is a set of questions at the end of each chapter to stimulate discussion and some ideas for practical activities for teachers wishing to explore the assumptions underlying their school's approach to discipline.

Chapters 4 to 5 focus on classroom discipline and concentrate on the similarities among the teachers studied in the different schools. Chapter 4 presents a framework for understanding teachers' classroom practice and discusses ways in which this might be used in teacher training and in helping experienced teachers pass on their knowledge to beginning teachers. The framework distinguishes two kinds of teachers' actions to promote and maintain discipline: the proactive, taken to avoid disruption arising, and the reactive, designed to 'nip trouble in the bud' and avoid a problem escalating out of control. The framework then goes on to describe the influences on the actions teachers take, the most notable being what they know about their pupils and the goals they have for the class. Details of what teachers did and the most important goals and other influences on their actions are given in Chapter 5.

Chapter 6 concentrates on the pupils' views of school and classroom discipline. It describes what pupils believe their teachers do to get the class to work well and reveals that a wide range of actions are seen as effective. As far as school is concerned, there is a surprising amount of unanimity among pupils about the rules which affect them most. Rules concerning freedom of movement around the school seemed the most salient to pupils, regardless of which school they attended. However, some differences emerge when pupils discuss sanctions and rewards, which in turn reflect the different kinds of expectations schools have of their pupils. This suggests to us that pupils are well aware of the assumptions that schools and teachers make about them.

Chapter 7 looks at parental involvement in both school and classroom discipline and suggests activities to investigate how this could be promoted.

Chapter 8 draws together the various influences on school discipline and shows how school and classroom discipline are connected. It contains a checklist of questions for senior staff to consider, drawn from the earlier chapters, and opens up the possibilities of a school investigating aspects of its own discipline policy and practice. There are now many texts offering advice to teachers wanting to research their schools and classrooms. Research can be an exhilarating, interesting and informative experience but, to be of benefit, it needs to be planned carefully. If, as we hope, teachers are encouraged to carry out research in their own schools, we urge them to take advice.

In an attempt to make the text 'user-friendly' we have avoided citing references to other authors, except where essential. A list of books and articles which we have found useful is given at the end of each chapter.

What is effective discipline?

We have already indicated that there is no universally agreed definition of what effective discipline is. It is, however, generally seen as having two distinct, if related, purposes. It is a means to an end, a necessary condition for learning, but it is also an end in itself. Discipline can be an outcome of schooling, socialising pupils into, for example, values of honesty, courtesy and regard for others. Interestingly enough, discipline as an end in itself was stressed far more by primary than secondary teachers. However, from the pupils' point of view, discipline was seen as essential for enabling them to get on with school work, rather than as a virtue in its own right. This raises some interesting questions about the school's role in social training which are touched on in the book.

There is agreement that what counts as effective discipline is heavily dependent on the context in which a teacher is operating. The age and stage of the pupils, the time of day, the time of year, the content of the lesson and many other factors can all have an influence. For example, what counts as effective discipline for a teacher working with a group of infants would be rather different from the discipline standard expected of older pupils. Similarly, what counts as effective discipline first thing on a Monday morning might be different from last thing on a Friday afternoon. So, the same teacher can have different standards of discipline; teachers in the same school can have different standards; and teachers in different schools can have different standards.

Where does this leave us in our search for effective discipline? First of all, it highlights the futility of the quest for a universal answer or magic recipes to deal with discipline problems. What is appropriate in one school will not necessarily be appropriate in another. To cite the Elton Committee's report on discipline:

> We find that most schools are on the whole well ordered. But even in well-run schools minor disruption appears to be a problem. . . .A wide range of causes of, and cures for, bad behaviour has been suggested to us. We conclude that any quest for simple or complete remedies would be futile.
>
> (pp. 11-12)

Schools have their own histories, their particular combinations of staff and pupils, their own cultures and circumstances which conspire to produce their particular approaches to discipline policy and practice. However, an understanding of how schools operate their discipline policy, and why they do so in particular ways, can sensitise us to aspects of school life that are perhaps taken for granted in the day-to-day hurly-burly. The emergence of similar influences on discipline policy among four rather different schools is suggestive of areas which schools could examine if they want to review their policy. Finally, schools need a starting point to review their policy and practice. Since effective discipline is such a slippery concept and varies according to context, such a review needs an anchor which will provide a line of enquiry but at the same time not be unduly constraining by suggesting a particular opinion. Our research was guided by the following strategic research questions. We list them here so that it is clear what concerns underpinned our enquiries of teachers and pupils in the schools we researched. The questions may also be useful to a school interested in researching its own practice.

The first set of questions concerned school rules and regulations. Work by many other writers had suggested that underpinning the notion of discipline was a concern with rules and adherence to them. We therefore wanted to ask:

- What are the school rules?
- What are seen as the most important rules in practice?
- Who decides when the rules have been broken?
- Who decides what happens to rule-breakers?

Since previous research on school discipline had indicated the importance of common standards in terms of rules, we were also interested in questions such as:

- Are common standards thought to be applied by staff?
- What factors are seen as affecting the implementation of common standards?

Finally, we were interested in the kind of support that the school could offer when indiscipline had occurred and in any measures designed to promote good discipline. This was translated into questions such as:

- Does the school involve parents in promoting discipline and in reacting to indiscipline? If so, in what ways?
- What kinds of punishments are used?
- How effective are the support systems perceived to be?

These were the questions which guided our enquiry into school discipline. For classroom discipline we used a more open approach. We did not want teachers to suppose that we had a predetermined idea of what effective discipline would look like in their classrooms. Nor did we wish them to think and talk about only punitive or authoritarian strategies. In our view, effective classroom discipline was something which allowed learning to take place. This was translated into a single interview question with teachers, 'What did you do to get the class to work well?' We were clear that effective discipline was not the same as effective learning. A teacher could have effective discipline without necessarily promoting and encouraging pupils to learn whatever was intended. Clearly, a teacher's knowledge about the topic of the lesson, the clarity and quality of exposition and the matching of these to what pupils already know and can do are all influences on effective learning. Can pupils learn if there is no discipline in the classroom? The answer to this must be that, at a minimum, effective learning is severely impeded if the teacher has little or no control over the pupils' behaviour. Effective discipline, it seemed to us, was a necessary, if not sufficient, pre-condition of effective learning.

It is important to distinguish effective discipline from effective learning if teachers are interested in researching their own classroom practice, so that the focus of their research is clear. Our approach was to concentrate on the actions teachers took and the influences on these actions. Teachers wanting to research their practice could note their actions with their class, for a small part of the day, over a few days. They could note the influence on these actions and the goals they had for the class and/or for individual pupils. Alternatively, a pair of teachers could work together, helping each other to describe their actions and the influences on them. Some ideas for using the framework to research classroom practice are given in Chapter 4. Our point here is that any teachers researching their practice need to be clear about which aspects are under investigation. Our approach was on actions taken to get the class to work well. We had no objective measures of whether the class did work well beyond our own observations. Our starting point was the individual teacher's definition. We can say from our observations that the pupils seemed busy and productive. The classrooms were enjoyable and interesting places to be and we witnessed no major incidents of indiscipline such as verbal or physical abuse among teachers or pupils.

Do schools make a difference?

Is our assumption that schools and teachers can take actions to affect the behaviour of their pupils well founded? The short answer is 'yes', although it is only in the relatively recent past that schools have come to be seen as social institutions, whose nature and climate have important influences on the behaviour, attitudes and attainments of pupils and, indeed, of teachers. Much of the recent research on school effectiveness has shown that schools do make a difference and that schools with similar pupil intakes and catchment areas can produce rather different results, not only in the academic achievements of their pupils but in the behaviour of their pupils as well.

Clearly, pupils' home backgrounds and their local communities are very important influences on their behaviour and values. We are by no means suggesting that these are neutral elements in a school's quest for effective discipline or, indeed, in other aspects of school life. However, it is more difficult for schools to influence their pupils' backgrounds and community culture than their own practice. There are things which schools can do to promote effective discipline.

Most of this book is devoted to what schools can do within their own boundaries. This is not to say that involving parents and the local community is unimportant; far from it. Towards the end of the book we suggest that schools could, with profit, examine their relationships with parents. Primary teachers had a great deal to say about parental involvement and its positive effects. Our own attempts to gather parents' views about effective discipline were fraught with difficulty and we did not have the resources necessary to allow home visits to interview parents, which would have produced systematic and reliable information about their involvement with the schools. There is overwhelming research evidence about the beneficial effects of parental involvement on pupils' learning. It seems that an important aspect of such involvement is in the values which parents portray about schooling. Schools, of course, have values too and these are reflected in their discipline policy. An important point for any school wanting to improve its discipline is to involve parents in the process. The vast majority of parents want their children to do well at school and to have a happy and enjoyable school experience. An important benefit of greater participation could be sharing of home and school values which, in turn, could have positive effects on discipline.

Before describing the schools' different approaches to discipline and the influences on their approaches, we need to say a little about the schools themselves and the way we collected information about their policy and practice.

The schools

The four primary schools were in two different regional educational authorities in Scotland. We chose regions and schools which were, in some sense, typical of Scotland. One of the authorities included a sub-division covering a large city which, in common with most British cities, had areas of multiple deprivation. The other authority contained a mixture of small and large towns as well as rural areas. Within these two authorities we wanted to choose schools which were, again, typical, but which would provide us with a contrast. How one chooses a typical school is a vexed question as all schools have claims to individuality and uniqueness. We chose schools largely on the basis of their size but bearing in mind our wish for contrast. In the city, the contrast was between a Roman Catholic school and a non-denominational school. The non-denominational school was in an area of multiple deprivation, while the Roman Catholic school had a more mixed catchment area. In the other authority, the contrast was between a school in a large and fairly prosperous town and a school in a small industrial town tied to a declining industry. We describe each of these in a little more detail below. For ease of reference we have given them fictitious names.

Westway

Westway is situated in an area of multiple deprivation – which has been described by teachers as 'Little Beirut'. The roll currently stands at 195, a drop of approximately a hundred in the past four years. However, the numbers in the early years are now increasing and a new nursery is being built as part of an urban-aid EEC project. There are nine class teachers, plus an assistant headteacher (AHT) early education (EE) and headteacher (non-teaching). In addition, there is a full-time auxiliary teacher and a permanent full-time learning support teacher. There are a number of visiting teachers for such subjects as music, art, fabric/craft and physical education. They visit fortnightly for two terms. The head and AHT were appointed approximately three years ago, and most of the staff have taught at the school for more than seven years. This is the headteacher's first appointment and he is very ambitious for the school. He follows a headteacher who was seen as having had a distant relationship with staff.

The school is open-plan and seen as very well resourced. Outside play areas are surrounded by grass. It is modern, carpeted, with large foyer area, glassed office, cafeteria dining-room and kitchens. The upper and lower schools are separated by the dining area and general purpose room. Each area – primary (P)6/7, P4/5, P2/3 and P1/2 – has its own exits/entrances and areas of playground. There has been little contact with parents to date, apart from the parent evenings which are generally well attended. An attempt to involve some of the parents in library-cataloguing and book-covering was halted after a complaint from the public employee union. The parental response to meetings connected with school boards (the Scottish equivalent of governing bodies) was extremely poor – six parents in total, and no board is yet formed.

The headteacher runs three clubs at lunchtime – chess, recorders and drums. He also has started a football club and runs this after school with a parent. Another teacher runs a netball team after school hours. There is little involvement with support services such as the educational psychologist. A number of the children are assigned to a family social worker. A recent HMI report on the school praised its positive approach, the high calibre of the work and the caring attitude of the staff.

St Veronica's

St Veronica's is situated in an old suburb of a large city. The suburb was once a village in its own right and retains a sense of community. The school itself is physically divided by a busy main road (there is a connecting underpass). There are two buildings; the more modern one serves P1, P2 and P3, and the AHT, early education (EE) and auxiliary teacher are based there. The other building is a red-brick, traditionally built city school where classes P4 to P7 are situated as well as the headteacher. Both schools have playgrounds surrounded by busy roads and houses. The school serves a very mixed socio-economic group, though the majority are reportedly 'stable working class'. A few children come from very deprived home backgrounds, with a still smaller number coming from child-care institutions situated in the area. This is a Catholic school which has strong links with the Church, which is next to the boys' playground (there are separate playgrounds for girls and boys).

The school roll currently stands at 205, a very slight decrease from 211 two years before. There were a few placing requests in 1989. Seven parents whose children were outside the school's traditional catchment area had opted for the school. The numbers at the lower end of the school are increasing. A purpose-built nursery is attached to the school, though only about a quarter of the children are taken into P1 from the nursery as this is non-denominational. There are seven class teachers and a non-teaching head and AHT (EE). There is a full-time auxiliary, who appears to spend most of her time at the lower end of the school. There are visiting teachers of music, art, and physical education, as well as a part-time learning support teacher. Most of the teaching staff have been at the school for more than ten years; some staff have experience only of this school. The headteacher had been appointed only a few weeks before the research took place. He has had experience of a number of different Catholic schools. His last appointment was at a Catholic school with, in his view, tremendous discipline problems, resulting in local authority intervention and regular pupil suspensions. He sees St Veronica's, in contrast, as having very few problems. Most of the staff would say that the 'disciplined atmosphere' was established by the recently retired headteacher with the support of the AHT (EE). This lady was described as a 'strong disciplinarian' who would tolerate no disrespect. The AHT was appointed more than fifteen years ago – in fact the headteacher was once a student teacher in her class.

The school – particularly the upper school – appears to be poorly resourced. The fitments and fittings are pre-1960s. There are very few extra-curricular activities, though the P7 teacher runs a football team, in which he also plays.

The headteacher has suggested that parents could become involved in providing some of these activities. Certainly, one of the changes which he plans is to increase parental involvement. A social evening organised for parents and staff was the first step. To date, parental involvement has been minimal. There are no obvious problems with pupil behaviour. Children are quiet, well-behaved and polite – they are 'trained' – boys to salute and girls to smile politely at teachers and adult visitors. This school has a school board.

Braidburn

Braidburn is situated in a small industrial burgh, serving a fairly working-class area. It is one of five primary feeders for the only secondary school in the town. The home backgrounds of the pupils are described as 'good', 'solid', 'well-disciplined', 'this is a very close-knit community'. There are a few families with serious problems of deprivation and neglect. The roll is static and stands at 227. There are nine class teachers and an AHT (EE) team teaching full-time with the P1 teacher. The headteacher is the only non-teaching member of staff. The school also has the services of an auxiliary and a learning support teacher, the latter for two and a half days per week. There is a stable staff, the last teacher appointed to the school more than six years previously. The headteacher has been in post more than five years, as has been the AHT. The school building was at one time split with the lower school housed in huts. Six years ago a new extension to the school was built and this is joined to the older part by a new 'spine'. The school is well resourced in terms of books and materials. Pupils have access to the open areas outside the classrooms where they work in groups on art and projects. There are visiting teachers in art, music and physical education and these are used on a rota system. Teachers felt that they required more time from specialist teachers.

There is much parental involvement and parents are visible in the school. Teachers and parents run most of the extra-curricular activities. There is a 'fun-club' and various sports activities run by the parents, as well as discos and barbecues. The Parent Association is very active and the school seems to be well used as an outside school hours community resource for the children. Teachers talk about the close-knit community and say that they value parent support. However, the school has as yet been unable to form a school board. The school also runs a house point system and the winning house receives a shield donated by a retired janitor.

The teachers feel that they have a well resourced and organised school. Staff explain that they have been working towards a more interesting and motivating curriculum and that this, in itself, makes a difference to the pupils' behaviour. Pupil entrances and exits to school are monitored by staff and pupil monitors. The playground for infants is near the car-park, separated by a low wall. The upper school has a separate playground, with another area for football. The playing fields which the school has use of are some distance away. The overall impression is of a school operating well and with children welll-behaved.

Oldtown

Oldtown is situated in an area which is very mixed, ranging from what is seen as a 'dump' for 'problem' families to large stone-built expensive homes with middle-class, professional parents. Of all four case-study schools it has the widest social range. Most of these pupils will go to Oldtown secondary school, to which this is the nearest feeder geographically. The school roll stands at 441 and is fairly stable. A third of the school roll is accounted for by placement requests. There are fifteen class teachers. There are three promoted posts, headteacher, AHT and Depute (EE). The headteacher and Depute have been in post four years, the AHT two years. The headteacher had had a previous headship post in another school. The AHT and Depute alternate each year in taking a class. There are visiting specialists of music, art and physical education, and a learning support teacher for two and a half days per week. Most staff have been in post a number of years and turnover is low.

The school was a targeted one during the teachers' industrial action a few years ago and both the extra-curricular programme and contact with parents appear to continue to be adversely affected by this. There appear to be no extra-curricular activities, though the school brochure claims that there are several. There is a Parent Association, but teachers feel that it is organised for and by the professional, middle-class and 'pushy' parents. The result is, according to staff, that other parents feel excluded. There is no school board.

The school building is an awkward one. It has a Victorian core with a late 1960s extension. It is mainly on one floor, though one of the P6s and all P7s are housed in an upper extension. The entrances and exits of pupils from the school are difficult to monitor because of the architecture of the building. This division of the upper school from the other stages also seems to create a dispersal of staff. The infant department's cohesion is achieved by the efforts of the Depute (EE) to bring them physically together. Some infant classrooms are at the other side of the building. Playgrounds around the school are also dispersed. The auxiliary supervises breaks. Oldtown's local reputation is that of a good academic school with few discipline problems.

Although the descriptions above convey something of the differences among the schools, summarised in Table 1.2, it is also important to draw attention to their similarities. They all taught the full age range of pupils from P1 (four- and five-year-olds) to P7 (eleven- to twelve-year-olds). They were over-whelmingly staffed by women, forty-seven women as opposed to seven men, and the average class size was about twenty-five although this concealed a range of size from fourteen to thirty-three. In two of the schools there was at least one composite class whereby children of, for example, P6 and P7 were taught in the same room. These then were the four schools whose discipline policy and practice we wanted to research.

How was information about the schools' discipline policy and practice collected?

To investigate school policy and practice we used the following approaches:

- interviews with a variety of teachers (details in Table 1.1);
- analysis of pupil's written comments about school rules, sanctions and rewards;
- analysis of school documents, such as the brochure, staff handbook and other material on discipline;
- the taking of notes on school life, often called 'field notes' in case study research.

Details about all these approaches, and about the ways in which we analysed the information collected, are given in the research appendix (page 131–8). For the moment all we need stress is that teachers in all stages of primary from first infants to upper primary were interviewed. We also interviewed senior management staff, an auxiliary, learning support staff and a supply teacher. The interviews were carried out in private, almost all were tape recorded and they lasted on average about an hour. In relation to classroom discipline, eight teachers were studied. We describe how we chose these teachers in Chapter 4.

Table 1.1: Numbers of staff interviewed

Headteacher	AHT (EE)	Depute	Teachers	*Others	Total
4	4	1	32	4	45

*Includes learning support teacher, auxiliary teacher and supply teacher

Two kinds of information were collected from pupils. First, we asked P6 and P7 pupils to write about what their teacher did to get the class to work well. Second, we asked the same sample of pupils to write about the school and classroom rules which affected them most, about an occasion when rules had been broken and the consequences of this. We collected data from 301 pupils in this way. In addition, where circumstances permitted, we conducted informal group interviews with younger pupils, ranging from P1/2 to P4/5. Sample details and more details on research methods are given in the appendix.

What can we learn from the intensive study of four schools?

Our study of four schools revealed rather different approaches to discipline among them, approaches which were seen as effective by the staff because of the kinds of schools they were. In the chapters which follow, these approaches are described and their benefits and costs are analysed. As important as what these schools did, however, is why they used their particular approaches. One of the benefits of an intensive study of a small number of schools is that it should be possible to discover the rationale for using particular policies. One of the most interesting things to emerge from our study was that, although the schools had different approaches, the same kinds of influences underpinned them – for example, the expectations each school had about its pupils. This suggests that schools wanting to review their discipline need to analyse many things which they necessarily have to take for granted in the day-to-day business of school life. For example, they need to analyse the expectations they have about their pupils by looking afresh at their brochures, at the kinds of rules which are seen to be important, the kinds of sanctions that are most frequently used and at the hidden messages conveyed by school documents, rules and sanctions. They also need to consider whether they have any rewards for good behaviour. It was striking to us that punishments for bad behaviour were much more in evidence than rewards for good behaviour.

The study of these schools, then, helps us to do two things:

- describe the different approaches to discipline used;
- identify the aspects of school life which need to be reviewed and examined before discipline policy and practice can be changed effectively.

We hope that the experiences of the schools strike chords about practice in your own school and will stimulate discussion and debate about why things are the way they are. It is very difficult to look at a familiar institution through the eyes of a stranger and to question aspects of school life that have to be taken for granted. It is also fascinating and enlightening.

It is similarly revealing and rewarding to analyse your own teaching or the teaching of colleagues from the starting point of what is being done to get the class to work well. There are so many reports of what teachers are not doing that they ought to be doing, that it is all too easy to neglect the routine, spontaneous actions which experienced teachers use to promote learning. As experienced teachers begin to play an ever more prominent role in the education of novices, it is surely vital that they come to understand their own classroom practice more fully and, indeed, how they came to acquire their expertise. Clearly, experienced teachers need to know about their own practice before they can pass on the elements of their craft to newcomers. This is harder than it seems, for the busyness and demanding nature of teaching do not encourage quiet reflection or discussion about practice. We hope that the framework for understanding the practice of eight experienced teachers, presented in Chapter 4, makes sense to teachers and teacher educators and is a guide to understanding the particular actions which teachers take every day in their classrooms in an attempt to get their classes to work well. We see it as being useful to teachers who have the responsibility of training new teachers 'on the job' as a way of making them aware of what they take for granted as normal classroom practice. We hope the framework is useful too, to teacher educators and local authority advisers in planning support for beginning teachers.

Finally, it can also be revealing to collect information from pupils about their view of school discipline. Many of the teachers in the case-study schools were sceptical about our attempts to collect information from their pupils. They were pleasantly surprised at the seriousness and thoroughness with which pupils answered our questions. Indeed, one of the best research experiences we have had was feeding back to teachers what their pupils had to say about their classroom practice. Obviously, it is more difficult for teachers than outsiders to collect information from pupils, particularly about classroom practice. Such an exercise would need to be carefully set up and explained. Perhaps it is more feasible for schools to collect information from pupils about their views of school rules, sanctions and rewards and the strengths and weaknesses of the school's discipline. They are an important and often neglected source of information about many aspects of school life. A small-scale pilot exercise with a couple of classes is a way of assessing the value of such an exercise.

Table 1.2: Characteristics of the four case-study schools

	Westway PS (non-denominational PS)	St Veronica's PS (Roman Catholic PS)	Braidburn PS (non-denominational PS)	Oldtown (non-denominational PS)
CATCHMENT AREA	• area of multiple deprivation, high unemployment • predominantly council housing	• suburb of a large city • village type community • mixed socio-economic groupings	• an integral community • area of declining industry	• suburban community • high levels of owner occupation • some council housing
SCHOOL ROLL	• under capacity • actual roll 195 (one or two placing requests)	• under capacity • actual roll 205 (7 placing requests for current year)	• at capacity • actual roll 227 (5 placing requests)	• at capacity • actual roll 441 (one third of the roll is accounted for by placement requests)
STAFFING	• above average to take account of pupil intake	• average (nursery unit situated within P1–3 building)	• average (nursery unit situated in school)	• average
HEADTEACHER	• first post as HT • in post for two and a half years	• HT recently retired after more than 20 years • new HT recently in post (six weeks) • HT experience in one school in difficult area	• in post for 5 years • first post as HT	• in post for 4 years • HT experience in different type of school

(continued)

Table 1.2 (*continued*)

BUILDINGS

• modern well-resourced open-plan building surrounded by grassy area	• school is 2 buildings divided by busy main road • P4–7 building housed in traditional red-brick, pre-war building • no playing fields beside school	• two Victorian buildings joined by modern, purpose-built extension • no playing fields beside school	• mainly traditional Victorian building with modern extensions added at different times • playing field beside the school

BACKGROUND

• declining roll • EPA school • area of planned urban renewal • PTA recently established • no school board	• declining roll • strong links with church sited next to school • PTA lapsed at time of teachers' industrial action • school board	• static roll • well-established and active PTA • no school board	• static roll • targeted school during teacher industrial action • good academic/traditional reputation • established PTA • no school board

References

Denscombe, M. (1985) *Classroom Control: A Sociological Perspective*, Allen & Unwin, London.

Department of Education and Science (1989) *Discipline in School*, (The Elton Report), DES/HMSO, London.

Docking, J. W. (1989) *Control and Discipline in Schools: Perspectives and Approaches*, Paul Chapman, London.

Docking, J. W. (ed.) (1990) *Education and Alienation in the Junior School*, Falmer Press, Lewes.

Gray, J., McPherson, A. F. and Raffe, D. (1983) *Reconstructions of Secondary Education: Theory, Myth and Practice since the War*, Routledge & Kegan Paul, London.

Johnstone, M. and Munn, P. (1987) *Discipline in School: A Review of 'Causes' and 'Cures'*, Scottish Council for Research in Education, Edinburgh.

Lawrence, J. and Steed, D. (1986) Primary school perception of disruptive behaviour, *Educational Studies*, 12(2), pp. 147–57.

McPherson, A. F. and Willms, J. D. (1987) Equalisation and improvement: some effects of comprehensive reorganisation in Scotland, *Sociology*, 21, 4, pp. 509–40.

Mortimore, P., Sammons, P., Lewis, F. and Ecob, R. (1988) *School Matters: The Junior Years*, Open Books, London

Peters, R. S. (1966) *Ethics and Education*, Allen & Unwin, London.

Reynolds, D. (1985) *Studying School Effectiveness*, Falmer Press, Lewes.

Reynolds, D. (1989) Effective schools and pupil behaviour, in N. Jones (ed.) *School Management and Pupil Behaviour*, Falmer Press, Lewes.

Rutter, M., Maughan, B., Mortimore, P. and Ouston, J. (1979) *Fifteen Thousand Hours: Secondary Schools and their Effects on Children*, Open Books, London.

Scottish Office Education Department (1977) *Truancy and Indiscipline in Schools in Scotland* (Pack Report), SOED, Edinburgh.

2
THE SCHOOL'S VIEWS OF ITS PUPILS

This chapter examines the different ways in which our four case-study schools promoted and maintained effective discipline and seeks to explain why they did so. It is not our intention to imply that one school's discipline policy and practice was more effective than another's: all were seen as effective by their staff. Their policies were different, however. The differences were evident in the kinds of rules which were emphasised to pupils; the ways in which sanctions were used when rules were broken; and the use of praise and rewards. Staff in each school saw discipline as being effective. A major influence was the school's expectations about its pupils. The key idea in this chapter is: *schools have particular and distinctive views of their pupils and this influences discipline policy and practice.*

This idea, that we, as teachers, define pupils in a particular way, may seem rather contentious. It may, for one thing, smack of labelling. We may be happier with the thought that schools use similar approaches to promoting good discipline and that they all see good discipline in the same terms. This was not the case in our schools, which differed quite markedly both in what they counted as effective discipline and in their use of sanctions and rewards. They were alike in their belief that it was the school's job to inculcate certain standards of social behaviour, in other words, that good discipline was an end in itself. Furthermore, they all believed that it was the school's job to set these standards.

It is also important to stress that the schools were alike in believing that they *could* influence their pupils' behaviour. It is easy to forget that it is only in the comparatively recent past, with the burgeoning research on school effectiveness, that school effects are becoming better understood. Research in the 1960s and 1970s in the United States attributed most of the variation among schools on outcomes such as attainment scores most directly to the social characteristics of pupils, particularly their home background and social class. These studies tended to underplay the difference that the school can make. More recent research, however, has demonstrated that pupil behaviour can vary markedly between schools with comparable intakes. The research suggests that what makes a school effective resides in that elusive phenomenon, school ethos, which comprises a combination of various factors. As we indicated in Chapter 1, our research had no independent measures of effectiveness. Our approach was to concentrate on what teachers and pupils saw as working well both at whole school and at classroom level. This chapter focuses on one aspect of ethos, the rules, sanctions and rewards systems in four primary schools which saw themselves as operating a largely effective discipline policy. However, we have no independent measures of how effective the schools were.

How did the schools view their pupils?

The schools saw their pupils in rather different ways, which seemed to be strongly influenced by their catchment areas. In Westway, for example, situated in an area of multiple deprivation, pupils were seen as likely to be lacking basic social skills. The school believed that home and school standards of behaviour were quite far apart and so went to considerable trouble to set out its rules and the reasons for them to their pupils. In contrast, Braidburn staff believed that home and school standards of behaviour were similar. They talked of their pupils as being just like their own children. There was far less explicit setting down of rules and standards of behaviour than at Westway.

All teachers have a great deal of knowledge about their pupils and many will talk about their abilities, foibles and interests in some detail. These descriptions and explanations are often good indications of the way the school defines its pupils and were important sources of information to us. In addition to informal conversation with teachers, we drew on the following sources of evidence to help define the school's view of its pupils and what it saw as effective discipline:

- the school brochure;
- written guidelines for staff on discipline;
- interviews with school staff;
- pupil questionnaires and interviews;
- general daily field notes.

All of the above sources are available to staff wishing to investigate their own school's view and we suggest some practical activities at the end of this chapter.

St Veronica's

It will be recalled that St Veronica's was a Catholic school which drew its pupils from a 'mixed' catchment area. The majority of pupils came from what teaching staff described as 'stable working class homes' but there was a small number of pupils who came from 'severely deprived homes where drug and alcohol abuse was common'. An even smaller number of pupils came from local child-care institutions. The school staff felt that their views of acceptable behaviour would not necessarily be shared by their pupils or their pupils' parents. Their approach was to lay down clear rules and specify the consequences of breaking the rules. These rules and sanctions were told to the pupils at the earliest stages and reinforced at regular intervals. They covered a variety of aspects of school life, ranging, for example, from standards of pupils' dress to the appropriate way to talk in class. Rules were expected to be obeyed implicitly and without argument or discussion. Respect for authority was a key element in what counted as effective discipline, as is evident from a typical comment from staff: 'We laid down the law with them and [made it clear that] these were the rules'.

The school made a point of setting out its rules and the expected standards of behaviour from the earliest stages. An example from a newly arrived intake of P1 pupils makes the point. The class was finishing pre-number work; some pupils had gone on to play in the Wendy House, others had plasticine and trays. The infant teacher walked around the classroom checking on the activities. The following interchange took place:

Teacher [to class]:	Right everyone. I want you to finish off your circus pictures now.
Teacher:	OK, Teresa? Is that the circus picture finished?
Teresa:	No' yet.
Teacher:	[with a long look at Teresa]: Pardon?
Teresa [smiling at teacher]:	Not yet, Mrs Brown.

This incident was discussed with the teacher after the observation session. She explains what occurred in the following way:

Teacher:	There was that incident when she answered me like that. She said 'No' yet'. Now she obviously knew that that was wrong because she knew immediately – *she knows how she should talk when she's speaking to me* [our emphasis]
Researcher:	Do they know that that's the expectation?
Teacher:	Oh yes, they know about how to talk in here. You know, if you hear them in the playground – the way they talk outside! But they know that there's a certain standard in here. I don't mean just in the classroom but in the school as a whole.

This small example illustrates, first, that the teachers knew that they could not take for granted their preferred language register in their classrooms and so had formulated rules about this. It also illustrates that these rules had been conveyed from the start to new pupils (the observation took place in August at the beginning of a new school year).

The explicit nature of the rules and their fair and consistent application was an important feature of St Veronica's policy and practice as we shall see later. Teachers suggested that clarity and consistency were especially important for those pupils whose discipline at home could be at odds with the discipline of the school. The emphasis of St Veronica's was on training the pupils towards an ultimate standard of behaviour in which respect for authority was a key factor. As this teacher suggested: 'I think we have an ultimate standard to set. We have certain beliefs and we try to emphasise these beliefs to the pupils'.

Rules were to be obeyed because teachers said so. Teachers were the people who knew best and any challenge to teacher or school authority was not tolerated. As Chapter 7 suggests, this respect for authority was also a key element in St Veronica's relationship with parents. The school was the authority and parents were expected to try to ensure that their children conformed to the school's norms.

Westway

At Westway there was a different emphasis on what counted as effective discipline. Although the school saw itself as firmly setting the standards of behaviour, it went to considerable lengths to explain the rationale for rules and to instil values in the children by encouraging them to think of the effects of their actions on others. Indeed, the school motto was 'Think of Others' and the headteacher through the school brochure encouraged parents to 'support the school in encouraging children to consider the effect their actions and behaviour have on others'. Rather than relying mainly on telling children how to behave, the staff believed that explanation alongside telling was a vital part in the personal and social development of children from backgrounds where it was assumed very different values counted.

The school was set in an area of multiple deprivation. The area itself was designated for urban renewal and had an unemployment rate far in excess of the national average. It was variously described, according to staff, as 'Little Beirut' and 'Steel Helmet Country'. One Westway teacher described it as 'a desert of deprivation' in which the school was seen as 'a little oasis'. Field notes taken on arrival and departure from school indicated packs of stray dogs roaming an area littered with debris.

The uptake of free school meals was considerably higher than in our other schools and school contact with social workers was far more common. Around 10 per cent of the pupils had family social work contact. The AHT (EE) described the procedure for contact: 'I have a note here in this book that shows who [which pupils] have social workers so that I know who to get in touch with. We're finding that we have quite a few at present'.

It was all these circumstances, the physical environment as well as the characteristics of pupils, which led Westway staff to believe that they could not take acceptable ways of behaving for granted. The consensus view among the staff was that: 'we do have this difficulty about different standards – one standard for home and one for here'.

An incident from the field notes may help to illustrate both the existence of different standards between home and school and the role of explanation in trying to convey different values to the pupils. One afternoon a P7 girl returned from the lunch-break, complaining to the teacher about some verbal abuse directed towards her by one of the boys in the class. She had been called names directed at her size and obvious physical development. While, normally, lunchtime complaints were dealt with fairly briefly, this incident was treated very seriously by the pupil's teacher. She explained in detail to the class why this type of behaviour would not be tolerated and explained the necessity of respecting the female pupils' privacy and treating others as they would wish to be treated themselves. It seemed to the researcher, initially, to have been a minor incident which was given an inordinate amount of attention. However, the teacher later explained informally during a coffee-break that she believed this type of female harassment was endemic in the home background of many of the pupils. The attention it was given was felt to be necessary if pupils were to be helped to break out of this pattern of sexual stereotyping. What Westway did was to make sure that pupils understood the reasons for the rules. These were spelled out in some detail and sanctions were applied firmly, consistently and with explanation. This explanation continued throughout all stages of the primary school. The staff's consistent approach was to encourage pupils to think about the effect of their action on others in terms of 'Would you like this to happen to you?'

At both St Veronica's and Westway the pupils' social background meant that teachers felt unable to take for granted what the school saw as acceptable forms of behaviour. Rules, therefore, had to be clear and explicit. Staff differed in the route they took in making sure that effective discipline was achieved. St Veronica's staff chose to 'tell' pupils very clearly about the rules. Westway staff chose the route of explaining in some detail the reason for the rules and the social effects of breaking them. As we shall see below, they also emphasised different rules.

Our other two primary schools had catchment areas which suggested to teachers that acceptable behaviour could be more taken for granted.

Braidburn

At Braidburn the school was viewed as an integral part of the community. There was much informal contact with parents and much of the school's extra-curricular activity was carried out by the parents. Pupils were viewed by staff as 'like our own children'. The general aims of the school as set out in the school's brochure emphasised the role of the pupil in the community and the school's responsibility in fitting the child to this role. The first of these aims is set down in the following way in the school brochure:

1. To prepare a child to take his/her place in society.
    In order to do this the school hopes to make the child:
    a. literate
    b. adaptable
    c. amenable
    d. courteous
    e. honest
    f. have a sense of responsibility towards other people and the environment

At Braidburn, pupils came from home backgrounds where discipline accorded with that of the school. The consensus view among Braidburn staff was that:

> . . . The children who come to this school seem to be from backgrounds that are more discipline-minded than other schools. Most of them are from home backgrounds where they [parents] would expect this discipline at home as well.

and:

> I do tend to think that the homes which the children come from have a strong influence on the standards of discipline in the school. Because there's no doubt about it that the children who come from homes where they know exactly where they stand and how to behave will come here with a discipline. As long as we ask them to behave, they will behave themselves exactly the same as they do at home, although there are some odd cases – a few odd cases – where perhaps they don't behave themselves, don't have the same standards.

School standards of behaviour were seen by staff as largely consonant with standards at home. There was, therefore, less explicit emphasis on the school setting standards than in either St Veronica's or Westway. It was assumed that pupils would know what counted as behaving well and would do so. The school's job was to extend and develop pupils' self-discipline, to encourage them to behave well for its own sake as an intrinsic good, rather than because the teacher was checking up on them. In Braidburn co-operative projects were used as a mechanism for developing children's self-discipline and for learning to work collaboratively with others of different abilities and skills. A major effort was also put into school-wide collaborative projects such as the school concert. This was a major event in the life of the school, involving all classes and teachers and many parents and even grandparents. In this school, teachers saw the possibility of developing a higher order of social training rooted in the values of the community as a whole.

Oldtown

Of our four case-study schools, Oldtown was identified as the one with the largest social range of pupils. Some pupils were from areas where families were seen as being 'in serious financial difficulties', while others came from relatively prosperous homes. Staff felt that most pupils came from home backgrounds where parents inculcated standards of behaviour consonant with those of the school. However, in the staff's opinion there was a sizeable minority of pupils whose parents did not share the same behavioural goals as the school.

A challenge for staff was to find a standard of acceptable behaviour which accommodated a number of pupils from a wide range of backgrounds. One member of the Oldtown staff described the pupil intake in the following way:

> . . . it's a very mixed catchment area. We have all strata of society. . . . it's getting them to gel . . . we get [pupils] from very large stone [built] houses to single parents in not very good accommodation. When a family has split up,

it's hard for the kids. I mean, you've got to come and go a wee bit because of the background situation of the children.

The school brochure set out a number of rules (fourteen) which covered aspects such as movement around the school, recording of absence and lateness, and boundary restrictions. Thus one way in which the school coped with the mixed catchment area was to spell out its expected standards of behaviour, even though staff believed that most pupils were aware of these standards from their parents. The brochure also described the school's methodology and curricular focus as 'tending towards the traditional'. Beyond the specifying of standards, it was more difficult at Oldtown to characterise the effect of teachers' perceptions of the pupils' home background on what counted as effective discipline. However, there was a slightly greater emphasis at this school on the discipline goal of a 'quiet working atmosphere' as a means to an end – namely, to promote effective learning. Teachers were given a high degree of freedom in obtaining this goal, perhaps a consequence of the school's larger size. The school had 441 pupils in comparison with around two hundred at Westway, Braidburn and St Veronica's. How this goal was conveyed to pupils was a matter for the individual teacher.

School differences in effective discipline: an overview

So far we have concentrated on what seemed to us to be important differences in the way the schools conceptualised effective discipline: St Veronica's emphasising a respect for and obedience towards authority; Westway's stress on explanation and the need for pupils to understand the rationale for rules and punishments; Braidburn's concern for self-discipline; and at Oldtown the focus on traditional academic goals and the need for a quiet working atmosphere. We shall see below in more detail the ways in which these rather different conceptualisations were translated into practice. For the moment, however, perhaps the sometimes subtle differences in emphases can be encapsulated by a brief illustration of two projects which were taking place in two schools at the time of the research.

At Oldtown, which valued a quiet working atmosphere, a drama production requiring the construction of a camel was taking place. One of the upper-stage classes was making the camel. This craft work was done within the classroom when pupils had finished their allocated work to the teacher's satisfaction. The end product was not displayed where other pupils could see it, but was stored in an office. At Braidburn, an upper-school class was doing an environmental study project focusing on flight. A model of an albatross was being built in a public area of the school. Other children from other classes were able to see and enquire about the project. If we remember that the goal of the school was to encourage pupils to work co-operatively in a self-disciplined way, this small example seemed to illustrate how the organisation of work fitted with this idea.

The most striking feature of the four schools, however, was not their differences but the dominant influence of how teachers perceived the social composition of each school's intake and the subsequent approach to school discipline. We do not wish to suggest that this was the only influence or, indeed, that teachers' perceptions of pupils' home backgrounds was necessarily accurate or complete. However, comment on pupils' home backgrounds dominated teachers' discourse on their schools' discipline policy and practice. Of course, primary school teachers have long been trained to cater for the 'needs' of the child and teachers' perceptions of these needs, at least in terms of children's personal and social development, seem largely to be influenced by assumptions made about the values inherent in the child's home. The ways in which teachers deal with mismatches between home and school cultures have been recorded by a number of researchers. Teachers may, for example, perceive pupils in particular ways according to the pupils' home circumstances. Research into the perceptions of teachers who taught junior school pupils suggested that they perceived pupils from unskilled manual backgrounds, and where father was absent from home, as having a higher incidence of behavioural problems. The dangers of labelling are clearly drawn from such studies. (Readers interested in this aspect of school culture will find useful references at the end of this chapter.)

The influence of pupils' background on teacher expectations of pupils has been a long-standing concern of sociologists. Opinion is divided on whether it influences teacher expectations and behaviour in the classroom. Our research concentrates on discipline rather than on the wider aspects of school and classroom life. Our data indicate that in our four case-study primary schools, what staff believed they knew about pupils' backgrounds was a major influence on the schools' discipline policy and practice. Let us now look at that practice in greater depth. First, we consider teacher–pupil relationships as a way of conveying school notions of discipline.

Teacher–pupil relationships

Establishing a 'good relationship' is commonly regarded as a basic prerequisite not only to classroom learning, but to good discipline. However, despite all the importance which is attached to it, the concept of a 'good relationship' continues to be an elusive one. For our own purposes we found Pollard's (1985) definition helpful. He suggests that:

> it is perfectly possible to analyse a 'good relationship' as a set of understandings which have been socially constructed through classroom interaction. The critical point here is that both teachers and pupils must recognise the basic concerns of the other.
>
> (p. 8)

Any relationship, of course, has to be continually renegotiated through daily interactions but the core or main emphasis of it generally remains intact. Pupil–teacher relationships are particularly important in the primary school. Unlike their secondary school colleagues, primary school teachers have contact with their classes all day, every day. Establishing conditions for pupils to work effectively is, of course, important to both groups. Primary teachers, however, seemed to us to stress the value of teacher–pupil relationships to a greater extent than their secondary counterparts. At all stages of the primary school, teachers talked of getting to know the children. In the classroom it was important for the teacher to get to know the class as a group and the individuals within that class and to build up a store of knowledge about them. In turn, it was important for the class to know the teacher and to understand his/her expectations. How these expectations were interpreted and conveyed depended on the school's view of its pupils and the discipline goals thought to be attainable. As we have already indicated, there were different goals in different schools. These goals defined what knowledge of the pupil was thought to be necessary and appropriate. They also helped to define the type of teacher–pupil relationship which would assist in achieving these goals. If these relationships were to benefit the school as a whole, teachers had to look beyond their own classrooms and come to an agreement with their colleagues on the type of teacher–pupil relationship most appropriate in their particular school. The greater the consistency among staff, the stronger the effect on pupils.

Let us consider the teacher–pupil relationships at Westway where the goal of the school was to achieve civilised social behaviour with pupils whose home backgrounds were thought to be largely deficit.

Westway teachers had agreed through whole school discussion that the best way to achieve effective discipline involved explaining the reasons for the rules and that the rules would be more acceptable to the pupils when conveyed by teachers who had established strong and positive relationships with them. Teachers also suggested that pupils, while often lacking basic social skills, also lacked confidence and self-esteem:

> [It's] the nature of the children. They are lacking in confidence and we have to try, in most cases, to build up their confidence . . . They are very easily put down so you have to be careful not to squash them flat. They could be really hurt by what you say or do to them.

It was important, therefore, to establish a secure and caring environment.

> It's important to build a good relationship with the children so that they can approach us for help with their problems. The children in this particular area require a great deal of attention and affection as this is often lacking at home . . . we encourage trust and a willingness to co-operate.

In practice, this meant that where reprimands had to be made it was vital that the relationship did not suffer seriously. As the following Westway teacher explained:

> Well, of course, there might be a telling-off or some sort of withdrawal of things they like. Mind you, after doing that I would be keen to build up the relationship again . . . I don't think it's a good idea to let that sort of situation go on. I think you've got to leave them feeling happy. I would try to make sure they understood that it was all over – they had been punished and now they were reinstated. These children in particular have to know that you care about them. You have to let them see this.

Positive teacher–pupil relationships were integral to making sure that West-way pupils worked well. It was seen by staff as a form of compensation for a deficit home background. Relationships were no less important at the other three schools; it was the emphasis of the relationships that was different.

At Braidburn, for example, there was not the discontinuity in standards which existed between home and school in Westway. This harmony between home and school standards of behaviour meant that teachers felt able to establish relationships with pupils based on a common code of conduct. They were allowed a certain amount of flexibility in finding an acceptable form of behaviour because teachers and pupils shared core values of acceptable behaviour. The teacher–pupil relationship could be described as facilitative rather than compensatory as it was at Westway. The following description of how Braidburn teachers established acceptable behaviour may help to illustrate this: 'Initially, when they come into the [class] room at the beginning of the year I give them as much rope as I can without letting them go too far'.

The teacher–pupil relationship and its relevance to effective discipline was very seldom referred to by the Braidburn teachers, whereas at Westway it was a central feature of their discourse. This, in itself, seems to suggest the taken-for-granted nature of the relationship at Braidburn. Teachers there did not feel that they had to make a special effort to compensate. The quality of the adult–child relationship was similar to that established in the home.

These subtle differences in relationships were also identified at our other case-study schools, at St Veronica's and Oldtown. These, too, were influenced by the teachers' preconceptions of the pupils' home backgrounds and the goals which were felt to be appropriate. At St Veronica's, the school's goal of respect for and acceptance of the authority of the teacher was reflected in the teacher–pupil relationships. This was described by staff as 'kindly but firm'. The operationalisation of this relationship was one where St Veronica's teachers treated pupils kindly and expected a certain respect to be shown by the pupils: 'When they're passing teachers, they must have nice manners and nice manners are . . . well, the boys salute and the girls – they will smile – just to show that we're there and that they see that we're there'.

In Oldtown, an appropriate relationship was more difficult to characterise, given the varying backgrounds of the pupils. With some pupils, teachers might see the need to compensate, with others – often those labelled as children with 'pushy' parents, for example – the teachers felt that they had to build a different relationship. In this school what was seen as an appropriate relationship could depend on the composition of the class.

This section has concentrated on the ways in which teacher–pupil relationships were used to convey school discipline. We now consider aspects of discipline, rules, sanctions and the use of praise and rewards in the school in more detail.

Rules

Teachers in the four schools described similar rules as being in operation. Rules which ensured the safety of the pupils, consideration for others and

respect for school property were most often mentioned. Variations in emphases, however, were clear. At Westway, for example, absence and lateness were
given a higher priority than in other schools, where the teachers suggested
that these were less likely to occur. However, Westway staff felt that this was
a feature which was likely to become a problem if it were not dealt with
quickly. The pupils' home backgrounds with relatively high levels of unemployment indicated to the staff that late-coming to school tended to be a
problem with a substantial minority of the pupils. As one Westway teacher
suggested to us:

> We have times when there is a lot of late-coming in the mornings. Because some of
> the parents are not working, there is no reason to get up, so everyone sleeps in. A lot
> of these children get themselves up. . . . Now, there's no point in getting on to the
> children. We would rather they appeared because when they are here they're in a
> super environment.

The school, however, felt that prompt action had to be taken to prevent
disruption to the pupils' learning. The lateness rule, therefore, was for the
parents as much as the pupils and it was strictly enforced. A 'late book' was
kept and after three occurrences the parents were notified and asked to come
to the school to discuss the matter. Good attendance was an important rule in
all our schools. At Westway, it was given particular importance because of the
social composition of the school intake. Teachers strove to demonstrate that
'home rules' such as sleeping late and unpunctuality were not universal rules
of social behaviour and consistently set out an alternative code.

In contrast, rules about attendance and punctuality were not prominent at
Braidburn because their importance to parents could be taken for granted.
Braidburn teachers suggested that rules should be flexible and capable of
being adjusted to a particular class or set of circumstances:

> I think once you're in the classroom, especially a new classroom, you can decide on
> rules within that classroom – and, also, the children can affect the rules. I mean, I
> wouldn't have the same rules with these children as I would for another class. I
> would have different rules.

Now, of course, all our teachers said that rules had to be flexible, but Braidburn teachers felt able to be more flexible because of the nature of the pupils'
home background. The rules at Braidburn were less fixed; they were adapted
to the particular situation. At Oldtown, teachers also felt able to be fairly
flexible about which rules were appropriate. These rules, however, had to fit
into the overall goal of a 'quiet working atmosphere'. The paths or routes
teachers took to achieving this goal varied from teacher to teacher and this
was felt to be appropriate given the higher number of staff and the pupils'
home backgrounds.

So far, then, what we have indicated is that rules were applied with different
emphases at each of our four case-study schools. We would also suggest that
this application of the rules seemed to be effective in these particular schools.
However, we could also speculate that there might be costs and benefits to
applying these rules in these particular ways. To take Westway as an example,

staff had decided that rules had to be explained clearly and the rationale given. The benefit for pupils was that they were clear as to the value of rules and recognised their justification. The cost was mostly in terms of the time resources which this involved, perhaps at the expense of other educational activities.

At Braidburn, in contrast, where rules were more flexible and applied as the situation developed, there were also costs and benefits. The cost may be more strongly felt by teachers who would have to continually monitor behaviour and redefine the rules. However, the main benefit might be to pupils, as long as they were able to understand that applying rules depended upon the particular situation. In other words, they would come to understand the rationale for applying rules.

Sanctions

A school's punishment system has been seen by researchers as an important factor which influences pupil behaviour. Some studies suggest that high suspension rates are linked with certain fairly fixed expectations of behaviour. Researchers have also pointed out that punishments can serve to alienate pupils from school and those in authority. Sanctions, therefore, it seems, should be used with care. It has been argued that punishment may simply teach children avoidance tactics and encourage them to behave only when an adult is present. What most research on classroom sanctions indicates is that for punishment to have more than a short-term effect it must help to convey to the child what matters morally rather than just what others expect.

Just as all our schools had similar rules for pupils' behaviour, they also had similar sanctions to bring into play when rules were broken. These ranged from warning looks and verbal rebukes for minor offences to lines, extra work and punishment exercises for more serious offences. For the most serious offences, suspension and, ultimately, exclusion from school were available. Evidence from the schools indicated that these ultimate sanctions were very rarely used. A single case of exclusion in the previous four or five years was the highest incidence of exclusion in any of the four schools. As with the rules, however, it seemed that the schools' conceptualisation of effective discipline determined both which sanctions were used most often and how they were applied. So, how did the schools' behavioural goals affect the sanctions used? We illustrate the differences by reference to two commonly used sanctions: the verbal rebuke and issuing punishment exercises.

The verbal rebuke

Teachers in all schools were expected to deal with the more minor classroom offences themselves. One of the most-used sanctions was the 'verbal rebuke', or 'a telling off'. We suggest that even this ubiquitous sanction was used in different ways in our case-study schools. For example, in Westway the verbal rebuke involved explanation of why behaviour was inappropriate, and expression of regret. In Oldtown it consisted of a straight telling-off with a reminder of the consequences for the pupil. We give examples of these differences below.

At Westway, where the teacher–pupil relationship was very important, the verbal rebuke involved letting the pupils know that they had disappointed the teacher by their behaviour; rejection and disappointment were vital aspects. As the following teacher explained:

> I will make a fuss if someone disappoints me with bad behaviour [I will] say 'I'm really disappointed with you. Why are you behaving like that? You're disappointing me, personally, because I like you and I don't want this to happen . . .'

Of course, predicated on this is that a strong relationship has been developed between teacher and pupil in the first place. Disapproval and rejection can have little impact if the pupil does not have strong attachments to the school and to the teacher. One way in which staff at Westway tried to ensure this was by providing interesting and motivating work so that pupils enjoyed coming to school. They suggested that school was a safe haven for their pupils; a place where they felt secure and confident in their teachers. As one Westway teacher described the school: 'they know they're going to come in to the same discipline every day – it's not going to change. Nobody's going to be drunk the next day nor are they going to be hit for something'. The school had established itself as a caring place, according to the staff. This view was supported by a recent Inspectorate report: 'The experienced staff work hard to foster and maintain a purposeful approach to learning and an orderly caring environment' (HMI Report, 1988).

Field note data and teacher interview data confirmed the particular register which teachers adopted in order to obtain certain behavioural goals. The verbal rebuke at Westway was a subtle one, conveying the teacher's sense of disappointment at the pupil's lapse in behaviour. The school's goal of developing civilised social behaviour was one, however, which required a thoughtful approach. Teachers talked of the importance of maintaining a positive relationship and developing the pupil's confidence, as we have already described. Care had to be taken to ensure that pupils understood that it was their behaviour that was being rejected rather than themselves. The type of verbal rebuke, though, conveyed a rejection of particular behaviour which was at odds with what was acceptable in school.

At Oldtown, the verbal rebuke was also used but in a different way. Acceptable pupil behaviour could be rather more taken for granted. Misbehaviour was not expected from most pupils. There was less need for explanation, as the following comment from an Oldtown teacher illustrates: 'I do give them a verbal warning and tell them that if I catch them once again they'll either be sent to detention or I'll give them a punishment exercise'.

The verbal rebuke at Oldtown conveyed to the pupil what the consequence of the offence would be rather than an explanation either of why it was wrong or the disappointment felt by the teacher. This latter route did not seem appropriate to teachers at Oldtown, given the nature of most of the pupils' home backgrounds.

Punishment exercises

All of the schools used this sanction more often in the upper stages, but with varying degrees of frequency. Westway staff seemed to use it very little:

> I don't think that as a school we use that form of sanction very much at all. For example, for a serious incident like fighting or spitting at someone it would be an absolute waste of time. You've got to explain why the offence was wrong – often the children don't know this. Writing out a punishment won't explain it to them. . .

Encapsulated in this comment on the value of the punishment exercise is the teacher's objective to get pupils to understand the rules before they can successfully internalise them. Such a view sits nicely with the view of pupil as deficit in social skills and of school as values compensator.

At St Veronica's, where the goal of the school involved instilling a respect for authority, the punishment exercise was seen as a sanction to be used when pupils failed to conform to school standards and to alter their behaviour after a less weighty sanction. St Veronica's teachers suggested that although it was necessary to take account of the child's background, school standards had to be upheld. This sometimes meant invoking the punishment exercise as a sanction in a fairly automatic manner. Pupils had to realise that rule-breaking would be dealt with fairly and with consistency by those in authority:

> I feel that we have to be made aware of those instances where home background does make a difference, but I don't think it's necessary that I be told all the details – I would take this into consideration, not just taking the child at face value. At the same time, if that child steps out of line, it's not always a case of 'Oh well, there are extenuating circumstances'. *The child is judged by what they have done, no matter what background they have – as far as I am concerned* [our emphasis].

Of course, teachers at St Veronica's explained the rules and made allowances for individual circumstances, but the importance of preserving respect for teachers and the authority of the school was the overriding emphasis.

The above two schools offered the strongest contrast in terms of how they used the punishment exercise to reinforce their behavioural goals. Our other two schools also used this sanction in line with the school's goals. Oldtown's more diverse goals meant that punishment exercises were used at the discretion of the individual teacher. As Chapter 3 indicates, the professional staff relationships at Oldtown meant that teachers were empowered to make their own decisions on which sanctions were appropriate. There were a number of reasons for this, the most important possibly to do with the larger size of the school and its dispersed nature. As an Oldtown teacher explained: '. . . it's impossible really for all the teachers to know all the children. Here it's more difficult. The classes are bigger as well . . .'

These aspects, together with the very mixed catchment area meant that Oldtown teachers felt that they made their own decisions according to what they believed would be successful on that occasion: 'Discipline is a thing that you've got to try to suit [to] each child, try to make the punishment fit the crime'. As far as the punishment exercise was concerned, teachers in Oldtown used it to suit their own classroom and pupil situation.

At Braidburn the punishment exercise was seldom mentioned by teachers as a useful sanction. They suggested that for the majority of pupils a reminder or verbal rebuke was sufficient to return them to an appropriate standard of behaviour. For those children who, for one reason or another, failed to adhere to this standard a timely report to the parents was often seen as a useful step.

Just as there were benefits and costs to schools in applying rules in particular ways, these were also evidenced in the application of sanctions. As other research has suggested, sanctions need to be used with care; otherwise there can be unintended consequences. One of the costs of applying sanctions in a routine, standardised way, as was the case at Oldtown, was that all pupils may not understand the fairness of the rules, or, indeed, may take an unrealistic view of the power of sanctions to regulate behaviour. However, when sanctions were applied in this way, it had the benefit of being seen as fair and consistent. It also meant that sanctions could be dealt with in a routine way, leaving teachers time for other matters. There are, of course, a number of costs and benefits of particular systems and it is for teachers and schools to decide which accords with their own circumstances.

Sanctions, of course, are only one way of ensuring that rules of acceptable behaviour are followed. Schools are also able to offer pupils incentives and rewards to encourage acceptable behaviour.

Rewards and praise

Research into the use of rewards and praise in schools suggests that teachers are sparing in the use of those strategies. Teacher educators and advisers encourage both of these as a means of promoting good classroom behaviour and a positive ethos in the school. An ILEA (1986) study indicated that where a school offered rewards this was likely to help foster a positive school ethos. However, the study indicated that when praise was used by teachers, its focus was on work, rather than behaviour. Further evidence from a recent survey of 900 pupils has suggested that a positive letter home from school to parents was one of the most highly prized rewards named by these pupils. It has also been suggested that rewards, like sanctions, should be used with care, otherwise there may be unintended consequences. Children might, for example, be encouraged to behave in a certain way specifically for the reward rather than for the intrinsic value of the activity. This detrimental effect of rewards on future behaviour has been demonstrated in a number of small-scale experimental studies.

The use of praise by teachers is also, according to research, comparatively infrequent. A number of authors have noted significant correlations between an increase in the use of praise and developing pupils' self-esteem. There is also a substantial body of evidence to suggest that school achievement is positively associated with the level of self-esteem. Once more, readers who are interested in this particular aspect of school practice will find the references at the end of the chapter helpful. Let us now, however, consider the use of praise and rewards as used by the teachers in our case-study schools.

The absence of rewards and praise in teachers' daily dealings in the classroom was reflected in our data. Our teachers did not talk at length or in detail about their use of rewards and incentives. We might speculate that this is because it is easier for teachers to talk about indiscipline and their reaction to this than to talk about how they rewarded good behaviour. The same was true at the whole school level. There were few system-wide rewards for good behaviour. One of the few which we came across was at Braidburn, where a house-points system was used as a school-wide incentive.

> We've got houses in the school and we award points for everything and anything, should it be neatness or politeness or kindness or whatever, or sports, or if they've tried really hard throughout that day – even though they weren't getting 'excellent' at all, but they've tried, then they get the points.

The house with most points was awarded a 'cup for merit' donated by the school's former janitor. This presentation was made during school assembly time, so that school-wide recognition was given to those in the winning house. The point of this example is that it seemed to us to illustrate the goal at Braidburn: that pupils should be encouraged to develop self-discipline within a co-operative approach. It was the role of the school to provide opportunities for them to do this. A range of behaviours appropriate for the individual pupil were therefore rewarded.

At Westway, teachers talked of a consensus among teaching staff to use praise inside and outside the classroom for good behaviour. As one Westway teacher observed:

> These particular pupils seem to demand a lot of love and attention. This involves a lot of praise. You must take a very positive approach. They [pupils] have little experience of rules and discipline, so it has to be done in such a way that they come to trust the teacher and the other adults in the school.

Praise was used to build up both the relationship between pupil and teacher and the self-esteem of the pupils. As another Westway teacher expressed the basic aim: 'We have to respect them if they are going to respect themselves'.

Westway teachers suggested that because of the particular catchment area it was important to encourage acceptable behaviour by praising this when it did occur. This statement from a Westway teacher was a typical one:

> They're all very eager for praise. [I] show them by my manner . . . by smiling at them, by patting them, [showing that they are behaving well] I do that a lot as I go round . . . [and I say] 'Oh, that's really super, that's great, that's better than yesterday'.

Are pupils aware of their school's views?

Our study has looked at discipline from a number of perspectives: teachers at all stages of the primary school, headteachers and the pupils. This chapter has suggested that teachers tended to emphasise certain goals for pupil behaviour rather than others. Were pupils aware of these goals? Our evidence suggests that they were, although it was clear that pupils had much in common as pupils, regardless of the school they attended. For example in writing about the rules which affected them most, the clear winner was any rule on out-of-bounds areas. Typical of the comment from pupils in all the schools was: 'You're not allowed to go out of school grounds. You have to play in your part of the playground . . . and not play on the grass when it's wet'. Clearly, being told where you are allowed and not allowed to be may have been more salient for them than the particular goals of their school.

Having said that, however, we also found, just as we had in the teacher data, subtle differences in emphasis. The teachers at Oldtown and St Veronica's, for example, were described by their pupils as more controlling than their Westway and Braidburn counterparts. But what does this emphasis tell us about the goals of the school? Oldtown's goal involved getting the pupils to work in a quiet atmosphere. The high number of pupils describing this need for quiet as an important reason for the teacher's use of certain actions or as an important classroom rule suggested to us that this was a goal recognised by the pupils. The following statement is typical of the way they described it: 'Our teacher shouts at us to make us quiet. If we are not quiet by then, then he says "I'll give you one more chance and if you're not quiet by then I'll give you lines".'

At St Veronica's, too, pupils seemed conscious of the restrictions of the school rules. For example, as one pupil wrote:

Not allowed to get the ball when it goes in ditch.
Not allowed to run in corridors.
Not allowed to go to toilet without permission.
Not allowed outside school gates.

There was also a greater emphasis on teachers 'being in charge' and establishing and adhering to rules. The pupils' acceptance of these rules involved the notion that teachers were accepted as the traditional authority. This element of respect for authority was, of course, an important goal in the school. This was not necessarily described in a negative way by pupils; it was obvious from the tone of the response that this was part of their expectations of their teachers. Different pupils in St Veronica's wrote that 'He lets you know he's in charge' and 'There are a lot of things you're not allowed to do. No running, no glass bottles, not down the ditch [out of the playground]'.

We suggested that at Westway the goal was to encourage pupils to accept the school's standard of behaviour through explanation and thinking of others. Teachers had explained that this type of behaviour was not always apparent in pupils' home backgrounds. They were conscious that pupils often had two different standards, one for home and one for school. To some extent this was reflected in what some of the Westway pupils said in informal discussion. The following extract may help to illustrate this. When asked about school rules, a group of P2 pupils explained:

Gregor:	Well . . . no fighting is a rule.
Cameron:	Yea, not in the playground or you get in trouble.
Michael:	I fight with ma team.
Researcher:	Do you fight in the playground, Michael?
Michael:	Naa . . . no' allowed . . . but after, I do.
Researcher:	After school?
Michael:	Yea, you're no' allowed t'fight in school but after . . . well . . .
Gregor:	My Mum says if someone hits, I've to hit them back . . .but we're not allowed to hit in school.
Michael:	Naa . . . so we do it after school. Then we can have a real fight with the [neighbouring school].

The above illuminates what the teachers described as the pupils' dual standards. Pupils had to be made to want to behave in what the teachers defined as an acceptable way. One way to do this was to get pupils to realise that discipline was a means to an end – enabling them to pay attention to the teacher and understand what work to do. As a different Westway infant group explained:

Susan:	Mrs Wilson doesn't like hairbands in school, see, 'cos when you're playing with it when teacher talks, well you don't listen.
Researcher:	So you should listen?
Susan:	Well, if you don't listen, you'll not know what work to do.
Carol:	And you do the wrong board sums.

We collected some data from pupils which indicated that they did internalise school values. The data are sparse, but important given the emphasis which schools place on transmitting the 'right' values. Interestingly enough, the pupils most likely to indicate their acceptance of school values outside school were from schools in more prosperous catchment areas, where, we can speculate, there was less distinction between home and school values and where school values were more likely to be reinforced by the home. For example, at Braidburn, where the goal of working co-operatively was emphasised, many of the pupils recognised the need for the older pupils to set an example. This Braidburn pupil lists the school rules and gives an indication of why they should be adhered to: 'Do not run in corridors, no glass bottles, eat your packed lunch in the correct area. Don't hit people . . . [They affect me] because it is up to me to keep these rules and show an example to the younger ones'.

It may be, however, that the pupil data tells us more about how it feels to be a pupil in general than a pupil in one specific school. We report pupil views more fully in Chapter 6. Certainly, pupils seemed to recognise that different teachers use different actions to get the class to work well, but 'working well' was very similar across the schools. There seemed to be an accepted need for an orderly working atmosphere in much of what the pupils across the schools wrote. The need for certain classroom and school rules in order to facilitate their own safety and the smooth running of the school, and to promote learning, was accepted. It was less clear whether there was the same acceptance of school discipline as inculcating societal values.

Conclusion

Our focus in this chapter has been on the notion that the case-study schools conceptualise effective discipline in different ways. While they all had the same broad goals of academic and of personal and social development for their pupils, they approached these goals differently. In St Veronica's, Westway and Oldtown, the expected standards of behaviour were clearly set out and conveyed to the pupils. St Veronica's emphasis was on telling pupils firmly and clearly what was expected and in inculcating respect for authority. Westway went to considerable pains to explain the rationale for its standards and to encourage pupils to think about the effects of their actions on others. Oldtown, the largest of the primaries, emphasised the goal of a quiet working atmosphere, but left it to staff to achieve this in the ways they thought most appropriate to them given their mixed intake. Braidburn, in contrast, took acceptable pupil behaviour for granted, did not spell out its rules and tried to develop self-discipline in its pupils. We have tried to show the influence of teachers' beliefs about their pupils' backgrounds on discipline policy and practice. In particular we have examined the influence on rules, mentioning, for example, the salience of rules on late-coming and attendance where pupils came from areas with high levels of unemployment, and the influence on sanctions and on rewards.

It is important to remember that we are not suggesting that some schools were more effective than others in their discipline. Indeed, our intention has been to try and describe different approaches to effective discipline. All the staff in the case-study schools saw their approach as effective within the school's context. Insofar as we have any 'objective' measures of effective discipline, such as suspension and exclusion rates, we have already indicated that across all the schools only one pupil had been excluded in the previous five years. This suggests that pupils were not in the habit of committing serious offences. Other indicators of effective discipline such as the HMI report on one of our schools and the views of teachers and pupils, show that the schools were not experiencing serious discipline problems. Our own observations over the eight weeks spent in the schools revealed no major incidence of rule-breaking or use of sanctions for the offences labelled serious and, indeed, the schools were welcoming and friendly environments in which to undertake research.

Each school's approach to discipline had benefits and costs and we summarise these in Table 2.1. We hope that by doing so we will stimulate discussion and debate among primary staff interested in reviewing their school's discipline policy and practice.

Table 2.1: Benefits and costs: teachers' expectations of pupils and of discipline

Westway	St Veronica's	Braidburn	Oldtown
Pupils lack social skills. Teachers can compensate for this by providing a discipline structure and giving reasons for good discipline.	Pupils are entrants into an established hierarchical system. Teachers can use the weight of the system to encourage good discipline.	Pupils are like us, like our own children. Teachers can build on community relationships to achieve good discipline.	Pupils belong to contrasting social groups. Teachers can encourage good discipline by emphasising the common denominator of work.

HOW DOES THIS AFFECT THE APPLICATION OF SCHOOL RULES?

Westway	St Veronica's	Braidburn	Oldtown
Rules have to be explained clearly together with the reason for the rule.	Rules are incontrovertible because they are set down by the teachers, the most powerful members of the school hierarchy.	Rules are generalised; they are both taken for granted and flexible. Rules are articulated formally as and when they are required.	Rules are stated clearly, but individual circumstances can alter how they are applied.
Benefits	*Benefits*	*Benefits*	*Benefits*
• Pupils may internalise the rules, rather than merely adhering to them. • Pupils recognise that rules are just.	• Pupils know the rules and recognise their own place in the hierarchy or rule system. • Pupils learn a routine of behaviour to encompass the rules.	• Pupils recognise that goals of behaviour depend on the group and the social interaction. • Pupils can see the rational basis for the kind of rule which has to be made explicit.	• Pupils are aware of the formal rules of the school. • Teachers are able to take into account the circumstances of the individual pupil.
Costs	*Costs*	*Costs*	*Costs*
• The time devoted by staff to explaining the rules may detract from other curricular areas. • Pupils must accept the teacher's rationale for the rules.	• Pupils may not understand the reasoning behind the rules. • Pupils may have unrealistic expectations of the power of the rules.	• Some pupils may not understand which rules are taken for granted. • Teachers may find this a very demanding situation in terms of constantly monitoring behaviour and redefining rules.	• Pupils may not understand that teachers are taking account of individual circumstances. Application of the rules may be seen as unfair. • Teachers have to consider carefully the circumstances of rule-breaking and the impact on other pupils of this flexibility.

(continued)

Table 2.1 (*continued*)

HOW DOES THIS AFFECT THE APPLICATION OF SANCTIONS?

Westway	St Veronica's	Braidburn	Oldtown
Teachers have to convey to the pupils that it is their behaviour which is being punished. They must also try to maintain the pupil's self-confidence. Teachers must use sanctions which convey these messages.	Sanctions are a routine, standard consequence of rule-breaking.	Sanctions vary to match the offence and the offender.	Sanctions are tied to work-type tasks but the diversity of pupils means that the application of such sanctions can be problematic.
Benefits • Pupils retain a positive self-image. • Pupils are not alienated by school sanctions.	**Benefits** • Pupils and teachers know the routine of sanctions. Offences are dealt with speedily and without fuss. • There is a clear association between the level of the offence and the sanction used.	**Benefits** • Teachers have more freedom and flexibility to apply sanctions as the situation demands. • Pupils can see that although there is an overall standard for group life, circumstances can alter cases. They recognise that offences and offenders may differ.	**Benefits** • Pupils see sanctions as objective and impersonal. • Sanctions are seen as standardised in terms of work.
Costs • Sanctions involving explanation can be time-consuming. • A high level of teacher skill and commitment is required to operate this system.	**Costs** • Teachers may feel constrained by the automatic nature of the sanction system. • Pupils may have unrealistic expectations that sanctions will change behaviour and be critical if they do not. • The rationality and fairness of the sanction may not be emphasised sufficiently.	**Costs** • Teachers have to agree that there is an underlying standard otherwise the system could fragment. • A minority of pupils may not be able to understand this flexibility. It could be interpreted as inconsistency or unfairness.	**Costs** • Pupils may come to see work as equating with punishment. • The rationality and fairness of the sanction may not be emphasised sufficiently.

(*continued*)

Table 2.1 *(continued)*

HOW DOES THIS AFFECT THE USE OF REWARDS AND PRAISE?

Rewards and praise are seen as essential to building up the pupils' self-concept and, thereby, their social skills. Rewards and praise emphasise the positive relationship between staff and pupils.	Rewards and praise are seen as peripheral, not used much because it is taken for granted that children will behave. Behaving well in school is viewed as morally correct.	Rewards and praise are used in different ways to suit the occasion and the pupil. Rewards and praise are used to build up group cohesion.	Rewards and praise are used to build up pupils' commitment to work. Rewards and praise focus on the idea that work is important.
Benefits • Pupils feel personally valued by the school. • Pupils take a positive view of the school.	*Benefits* • Pupils learn to behave without extrinsic rewards.	*Benefits* • Pupils see school as a good place to be. • Pupils develop a group identification with the school.	*Benefits* • Work is seen as important. • Pupils are encouraged to work.
Costs • Teachers have to take care that work is not sacrificed for time taken building up teacher/pupil relationships.	*Costs* • Pupils may not feel valued by school. • School can become a drudge and a bore.	*Costs* • A feeling of unhealthy group rivalry may develop. Less successful groups may feel undervalued. • Senior staff time has to be spent in organising composition of 'house groups' to achieve a balance across the school.	*Costs* • Pupils who do not achieve may not feel valued by school. • Some children may never be rewarded.

So far we have concentrated on one influence, to us the major influence, on what schools count as effective discipline: the social composition of the pupil intake. However, this was not the only influence and Chapter 3 considers another important area: relationships between the headteacher and staff and relationships among the staff.

Investigating your own school's view of its pupils

Looking at our own practice is no simple task. We all become so familiar with our practice and our surroundings that it is difficult to look at these objectively. The following questions and activities may help to focus on aspects of discipline in your school.

- Analyse the school brochure. Check up on what it says about rules, sanctions, and rewards. What messages do these convey about effective discipline?
- Check your interpretation of the brochure with colleagues. If there are disagreements about the messages in the brochure does this reveal ambiguity in the brochure's language, or different staff views of what counts as effective discipline?
- If there are areas of mismatch between the brochure and school intentions what can be done to improve matters? Is there need for more than a re-drafting of the brochure? For example, do staff need to debate and discuss school rules, sanctions and rewards, and re-think them?
- Are there any rewards for good behaviour in your school? Is there a school-wide system? How widely is this system used? Discuss this aspect with a group of colleagues to find out.
- Look at the benefits and costs table for the four schools. Do they strike chords with your own situation? What would be the benefits and costs of any changes to rules, sanctions and rewards?

References

Brophy, J. (1987) Socialising students' motivation to learn, in M. L. Maehr, and D. A. Kleiber, *Enhancing Motivation*, JAI Press, Connecticut.

Chang, T. S. (1976) Self concepts, academic achievement and teachers' ratings, *Psychology in the Schools*, 13, pp 111–13.

Coleman, J. S., Campbell, E. Q., Hobson, C. J., McPartland, J., Mood, A. M., Weinfield, F. and York, R. L. (1966) *Equality of Educational Opportunity* (Coleman Report), United States Government Printing Office, Washington.

DeCharms, R. (1976) Motivation Enhancement in Educational Settings, in R. E. Ames, and C. Ames, (eds.) *Research on Motivation in Education, Volume 1: Student Motivation*, Academic Press, London.

Docking, J. W. (1987) *Control and Discipline in Schools: Perspectives and approaches*, Second Edition, Paul Chapman, London.

Gill, M. P. (1969) *Patterns of Achievement as Related to the Perceived Self*, American Educational Research Association, Washington DC.

Grunsell, R. (1980) *Beyond control? Schools and Suspension*. Writers & Readers, London.

Gurney, P. W. (1990) The enhancement of self esteem in J. W. Docking, (ed.) op cit.

Hargreaves, D. H. (1967) *Social Relations in a Secondary School*, Routledge & Kegan Paul, London.

HM Inspectorate (Scotland) (1989) *Effective Primary Schools*, HMSO, London.

Holt, J. (1969) *How Children Fail*, Harmondsworth, London.

Inner London Education Authority (1986) *The Junior School Project*, ILEA Research and Statistics Branch, London.

Jencks, C., Smith, N., Acland, H., Bane, M. J., Cohen, D., Gintes, H., Heynes, B. and Michaelson, S. (1972) *Inequality: A Reassessment of the Effect of Family and Schooling in America*, Basic Books, New York.

King, R. (1978) *All Things Bright and Beautiful?* Harmondsworth, London.

Lawrence, J. and Steed, D. (1986) Primary school perception of disruptive behaviour, *Educational Studies*, 12(2), pp 147–57.

Mortimore, P., Sammons, P., Lewis, F. and Ecob, R. (1988) *School Matters: The Junior Years*, Open Books, London.

Nash, R. (1976) *Teacher Expectations and Pupil Learning*, Routledge & Kegan Paul, London.

Pollard, A. (1985) *The Social World of the Primary School*, Holt, Rinehart & Winston, Eastbourne.

Purkey, W. W. (1970) *Self Concept and School Achievement*, Prentice-Hall, New York.

Reynolds, D. (1976) The delinquent school, in M. Hammersley, and P. Woods, (eds.) *The Process of Schooling: A Sociological Reader, Routledge & Kegan Paul/ Open University Press, London.*

Rutter, M., Maughan, B., Mortimore, P. and Ouston, J. (1979) *Fifteen Thousand Hours: Secondary Schools and their Effects on Children*, Open Books, London.

Scottish Office Education Department (1977) *Truancy and Indiscipline in Schools in Scotland* (Pack Report), SOED, Edinburgh.

Sharp, R. and Green, A. (1975) *Education and Social Control: A Study in Progressive Primary Education*, Routledge & Kegan Paul, London.

Simon, W. E. and Simon, M. G. (1975) Self esteem, intelligence and standardised academic achievement, *Psychology in the Schools*, 12, pp. 97–9.

Whedall, K. and Merrett, F. (1988) Which classroom behaviours do primary school teachers say they find troublesome? *Educational Review*, 40, 1, pp. 13–28.

Willis, P. (1977) *Learning to Labour*, Saxon House, London.

Winkley, D. (1990) The management of children's emotional needs in the primary school, in J. Docking, (ed.) op cit.

3
STAFF RELATIONSHIPS AND DISCIPLINE

In this chapter we look at how relationships between members of staff in primary schools can work to affirm and sustain good discipline. The key idea is that: relationships are the basis of a support network which helps teachers to maintain good discipline.

What do we mean by relationships? Social and personal relationships are important, as we shall see later, as are relationships with pupils and with their parents. The latter are discussed elsewhere, in Chapters 6 and 7. Our focus in this chapter is on the managerial relationship and on the relationship between professional colleagues. What makes these of key importance to the primary school is very simply the smaller size of the average primary school.

The 'management team' in the primary school is perhaps the headteacher and an assistant headteacher with responsibility for early education, colloquially and historically known as 'the infant mistress'. In larger schools this team may be extended to consist of headteacher, depute head and assistant head. In either situation it is probable that only the headteacher will have no teaching responsibility; this, too, depends upon school size. In many smaller primary schools, headteachers accept responsibility for teaching a particular class and almost all primary headteachers teach classes in their school from time to time. Indeed, their practical involvement in the day-to-day business of teaching is an important element in their promotion of good discipline. There are not, of course, the different layers of management in a primary school that are found in a secondary school, where discipline is dealt with by class teachers, heads of subject departments, pastoral care specialists, the assistant headteacher(s), the deputy head and the headteacher. In the secondary school these many layers have led management to produce not just policy papers on good discipline, but guidelines on how (and on what offences) to move on upwards through the referral chain, as our own case studies in our companion volume on secondary schools showed. The complexity of this layered system may seem bureaucratic and paperbound but, in practice, it can provide secondary school teachers with a degree of choice of whom to consult with a problem. It can also be a way of distancing the classroom teacher from the most senior staff.

There are no formal layers of management to distance teachers from the senior management team in the primary school. Each party is more visible and more exposed than in the secondary school. We would suggest that this affects this collective task of education and places greater weight on the management–staff relationship. This is something of which you may be aware in your own school, that the relative visibility of management to teachers and teachers to management requires the investment of time and thought if positive management–staff relationships beneficial to the school are to be built.

In addition to relationships with management, we suggest that teacher-to-teacher relationships are of importance to good discipline. This is something which emerged in the departmental context in the secondary school. The department was the first (if not necessarily the only) potential source of support and help for teachers. Primary school teachers are unlikely to be divided into subject-specialist groupings. They are more likely to have direct everyday contact with their colleagues as well as with management, and to rely on less formal ways of communicating ideas. Again, this is something which you may recognise from your own school as important to co-operation and to work goals.

The role of the headteacher and management team

The smaller size of the primary school is no guarantee that the role of the headteacher is in some sense easier. In fact, the relative lack of other levels of management may put greater pressure on the primary school headteacher, who may feel responsible for determining the ethos of the school and for persuading or leading teachers into agreement. To the parents or to the public at large, the primary school headteacher may be solely (and visibly) accountable for what is seen as the success or failure of the school.

Small management teams were a feature of our case-study schools. In three schools the management team consisted of the headteacher and an assistant headteacher who was in each case head of early education. In Oldtown, the largest of the schools, the team consisted of a headteacher, a depute headteacher and an assistant headteacher. The depute headteacher in Oldtown was in charge of early education. In Braidburn and Oldtown the assistant headteachers had virtually full teaching timetables, thereby restricting opportunities to develop fully a management role.

Dealing with indiscipline was the most visible disciplinary role of management, and one which was praised by staff in all the four schools. Teachers of classes in the middle or upper primary school tended to look to the headteacher for this kind of support. Teachers of infants looked to the AHT/

depute (early education). Support was given by management in the passing, or as a formal, official sanction. Both kinds of support were welcomed, as the teachers noted:

> Even before 'official' support is required, in fact we'd just mention it maybe in the staff-room or Mr [the headteacher] might be in the [teaching] area, [and] he might hear me going on at someone. He'd come in and say, 'Oh, is he being a pest?' It immediately shows authority and that he's there to support me.
>
> (Teacher, Westway)

> Well, Mrs [AHT] she does back you all the way, she's very good . . . It's not something you do constantly, always sending them to her door.
>
> (Teacher, St Veronica's)

> The headteacher's the ultimate [sanction] . . .! Yes, therefore I rarely use [her]. Not that she'd want to be seen first as [a stern disciplinarian] . . . but there has to be someone overall in charge.
>
> (Teacher, Braidburn)

> When it gets more serious, it's handed along to Mrs [AHT]. They all seem to like [her], but at the same time have a certain fear, no, awe, of her.
>
> (Teacher, Oldtown)

In all four schools, pupils saw 'being sent to the headteacher' as the most serious sanction applied to disciplinary offences (see Chapter 6), but the headteachers' use of their power varied. In Oldtown, the headteacher had initiated a detention system for which she took responsibility. This seemed to be an attempt to formalise, and make public, school disapproval of 'bad' behaviour. In the other schools, the headteacher's role in applying sanctions was less formalised and more taken-for-granted. The benefit of the formal affirmation of the headteacher's involvement in discipline problems was that teachers did recognise managerial support. The cost was that any disagreement about who to send to detention and why, and disagreement about what pupils should do in detention, brought teachers and management into dispute as to the best procedure.

In general, back-up from the headteacher and/or head of early education served to affirm 'good discipline' in the particular school. In this context the AHTs/depute headteacher had a well-defined leadership role. Their expertise in early education meant that their specialist knowledge and skills were drawn on to implement the school's discipline standards. In our four schools, without exception, all the teachers of infants saw it as their task to train the children into the correct ways of behaving for their particular school. The AHTs and depute were, therefore, an important source of information and help on what that training should consist of and how to go about achieving it. This was a very important and powerful role for those in charge of early education. It was a role, however, which was dependent on consultation and discussion with the headteacher. None of the headteachers relinquished the early setting of standards to the in-house expert, although they recognised the vital importance of the infant stage for school discipline. As the headteacher in Westway said:

> . . . you look back and remember children sitting under desks crying and throwing

sand around. Now we look at the way they line up for dinners, the way they can come to a service and sit there for twenty minutes . . . The school rules are learned at this stage . . . the children know the kind of discipline that's expected of them.

As we shall see below, each of the headteachers participated in and contributed to this crucial stage of standard setting although it was the AHT/depute, through her teaching of the infant stages, who played a leading role in operationalising correct standards by her classroom techniques. In many ways this role was emphasised by the fact that the infant department in all the schools was physically separate. The infants had their own entrance to the school and their own playground. Of course, the separation of infant pupils could have negative results. For example, the teachers could see themselves as forming two separate groups, each of which might view the other initially as having different standards of discipline. The depute/AHT (early education) had a distinctive role to play inside the school and in being first contact with parents at the school gates. However, the headteachers had the central role in embodying the ethos of the school by setting overall standards of discipline and in conveying these to parents and pupils and to various official outsiders such as educational psychologists, social workers and college lecturers. Let us consider the more subtle business of the role of the headteachers in developing good professional relationships with their staff which helped to promote and sustain discipline.

As already mentioned, one way in which the headteachers did this was to deal with indiscipline and to offer support and advice to the staff. The headteachers also tended to be highly visible around the school – sometimes 'looking in' informally in a class, at other times teaching. On occasion this might be as help in an emergency, but there were also instances of headteachers deliberately joining a teacher in order to help achieve the desired standard of pupil discipline. For example, the new headteacher in Westway had established a habit of seeing all the classes, of doing a little teaching with each class, in conjunction with the class teacher. This strengthened the managerial–teacher relationship and emphasised to the pupils that all the adults had the same expectations. It also allowed the headteacher to give tactful help to a probationer teacher having difficulties. This teacher did not feel singled out by the presence of the headteacher, who was able to demonstrate to the probationer what was expected of pupils – and of teachers – in Westway. In the same way, the headteacher at Braidburn helped one of the teachers with a class acknowledged throughout the school as difficult. This class was seen as not 'gelling', not being a class, and as not sufficiently committed to working. In this case, teacher and headteacher discussed possible ways of co-operative teaching, tried out the ideas, altered their plans and generally experimented with ways to achieve what both agreed was the correct discipline for Braidburn.

In both these examples, the headteacher made visible what was expected in that specific school, and also emphasised that the co-operative relationship between management and teachers was valued. The support given by management to teachers seemed to result in a reciprocal loyalty, a relationship where most people felt they were on the same side. The point of being on that same side was to see through a certain standard of behaviour appropriate for 'our school'. The message given to the pupils was that the adults took the same view of discipline. The benefits of visible headteacher participation and intervention seem clear, but the real effect of participation and intervention was mediated by the relationships in the school. We return to this point later.

Interestingly enough, few of our teachers spoke of the headteacher's role in setting out a discipline policy, although in fact each school had such a policy. The existence of a formal, written discipline policy was acknowledged chiefly in Westway, where the new headteacher had been circulating papers to the staff. In all of the four schools, there was a taken-for-grantedness about defining good discipline, as far as the staff were concerned. This puts discipline in proportion, as only part of the teachers' concern for their pupils. However, we wondered whether the teachers in any one of the four schools were all taking the same things for granted. The elements of good discipline were defined rather differently in each school, but teachers within each school thought they knew and agreed on what was acceptable, in an informal, commonsense way. Their conclusion was based on the relationships in the school and on how management acted, rather than on formal, written policies.

Differences among the schools

So far we have concentrated on the similarities among the schools in the role adopted by the headteachers in promoting discipline and in the importance of the role of the AHT/depute (early education) in implementing the schools' standards of discipline. There were three main differences, however, in management approaches which are worth drawing attention to. These are in the wider responsibilities given to AHTs, the amount of freedom for teachers to set their own discipline standards in the classroom and in perceptions of pupils. We deal with each of these in turn.

The role of the AHT

As mentioned earlier, the AHTs in St Veronica's, Braidburn and Westway were all experts in early education and they all played similar roles in affirming school standards in the infant department. Beyond this, however, their roles differed somewhat. In St Veronica's, the recently retired head made it clear that he had no expertise in early education and expressly delegated responsibility for this stage to the AHT. He also made it clear that she was expected to deal with 'girls' problems' throughout the school. The latter was a role the AHT had traditionally played and was happy to continue. Furthermore, the fact that the infant department was contained in a separate school building perhaps encouraged the clear delegation of responsibility to the promoted member of staff in that department. In contrast, the head in West-way, an open plan school, adopted a policy in which responsibility for infants was shared. The head was often to be seen in the infant department, for example, an event that would have been unusual in St Veronica's. The AHT in Westway was expected to and did contribute to strategic planning for the infant department but in a more directly collaborative way.

In Braidburn, the AHT tended not to see herself as having a management role, but rather as an expert and experienced infant teacher who was avail-able, ready and willing to help her colleagues teaching infants on such matters as teaching methods and curriculum development. She saw herself as a spe-cialist adviser to the headteacher, but did not see it as appropriate to be part of strategic decision making on policy. This was understandable, as she had a full teaching timetable as a class teacher.

In Oldtown, our only male AHT had responsibility for work in the upper primary (the depute headteacher was an infant specialist). He had a half day per week from class teaching to catch up on paperwork, keep abreast of developments in curriculum and assessment and generally act as an adviser to teachers of the upper primary. He had no direct role in discipline policy as a manager.

We have no firm evidence about how or why these roles developed in rather different ways. We can only speculate that in many ways they were consistent with what the school counted as effective discipline. In St Ver-onica's, an explicit respect for authority and recognition of hierarchy perhaps encouraged a line management approach to the role of AHT. In Westway, the emphasis on openness and sharing, which was operationalised to the pupils as painstaking explanation of the rationale for rules, was consistent with close day-to-day collaboration between the headteacher and AHT. In Oldtown and Braidburn, the pragmatic constraints of the timetable perhaps provide more ready explanations for differences than policies on discipline. However, the depute headteacher in Oldtown had considerable autonomy on how to oper-ationalise her role, an autonomy also evident in teaching staff. This in turn may have limited the extent which the AHT could team teach or offer advice to colleagues in the upper school. It seems to us that the role of primary AHT as manager needs further investigation. This is something which different schools may see differently. In your school, do you consider that the skills of the deputy headteacher or AHT are being put to maximum use? What is this person's contribution towards discipline in the school?

Restricted freedom as support

All the headteachers saw it as their responsibility to provide help and support in instances of pupil indiscipline and, more generally, to take the lead in setting standards of good discipline. However, there were important distinc-tions among our schools in terms of the kind of managerial relationship operating. These distinctions had consequences for discipline in the school overall. One of the most important distinctions was in the degree of restriction placed on teacher autonomy, as we noted briefly in the preceding section. The picture of how teachers and management agreed on management's supportive role conceals the restrictions placed upon teacher freedom of action. It was not the case that the classroom teacher could adopt his or her own definitions of good discipline and then call upon support from management if trouble arose. Although taken for granted, or thought to be informally arrived at, a policy on good discipline existed in our four schools, as we saw in Chapter 2. The existence of this policy, however loosely defined, set limitations upon the teachers and restricted their freedom of action. The reward for accepting this restriction was support from management.

Teachers did not disagree with the headteacher's policy as they saw it. Although in each school there was at least one person who had some queries or doubts, the teachers recognised that aspects of their professional role were defined by the head. As one teacher in Braidburn put it (in describing the discipline policy of all teachers reprimanding any pupil seen misbehaving anywhere in the school): 'That's something the headteacher wants. We know that, the whole staff knows that'.

If management is to advocate successfully a policy on good discipline, one of the essential factors must be a degree of co-operation from the teachers to ensure consistency across classrooms. In a large secondary school, with seventy or eighty staff members, non-co-operation on principle (e.g. a teacher's disapproval of the wearing of uniform as a school rule demonstrated in not penalising pupils who 'forget' it) or non-co-operation out of disaffection (e.g. 'it's not my job' to patrol corridors) might easily exist, especially if support groups of like-minded staff are available. In a small primary school with a staff of eight upwards, non-co-operation could be more difficult to sustain if management and most colleagues are united in pursuing a particular policy and are seen to apply consistent standards in the everyday life of the school. In a small group, to agree with the group might be a more comfortable position to adopt. At the risk of being facetious, we could call this the stout corset theory of group action. Those who accept the corset of school policy or standards may be restricted – but they are also well supported. And, of course, a corset is not a strait-jacket. How did our four schools stand on restricted autonomy?

In Oldtown the relationship between staff and the headteacher was compartmentalised. By this we mean that within the school there were a number of separate groupings. The infant teachers turned to the depute headteacher for managerial support and advice. She in turn advised the headteacher. Teachers in the upper school formed a loose alliance with the AHT, to tackle any problems or common concerns. The AHT in turn formed part of the managerial advisory group. Teachers who taught the intermediate classes had no managerial voice or spokesman, but they had one another for support. These three basic teacher groupings were managed in such a way that teachers had some degree of freedom to define their own boundaries of acceptable pupil behaviour. For example, the teachers of the upper primary classes made their own decisions about keeping good discipline in their area of the school. One teacher gave an example of this: The [upper primary staff], got together and said [the pupils] had better behave on the stairs, so that was [how the stair rules were set up]. I think it's just common sense, the rules in the school.

In Oldtown, there seemed to be less day-to-day informal contact between the headteacher and the staff. More formal contact, in terms of taking over a class or forming a class, occasions for the headteacher to demonstrate and reaffirm 'good discipline in our school', took place in one of the groupings, one of the compartments of this school. This larger school did generate more paperwork, and it was also the case that the physical layout of the building separated the headteacher's office from passing casual sight of the staff, as well as separating infants, intermediate and upper primary classrooms. In Oldtown, the headteacher was seen as supportive in discipline matters, but this was a support rarely called upon. The benefit of the more compartmentalised management–staff relationships was that a degree of autonomy and professional independence was given to teachers. Their sponsorship of good discipline was firmly based on what they saw as suiting their particular classroom or stage of the school. The cost was that managerial vigilance and skill were required, to ensure that this autonomy did not become independent from the standards appropriate to the school as a whole.

In the other three schools, teacher freedom to act was more readily acknowledged as restricted, but we should stress that this was not seen by staff as an imposition:

> We always discussed things and came to some sort of agreement [about rules] but it was never written down.
>
> (Teacher, St Veronica's)

> We all seem to have the same frame of mind, it just happened like that.
>
> (Teacher, Braidburn)

> We work together. I think that's one thing you do notice, we sort of agree together. We get on well and share the same set of views.
>
> (Teacher, Westway)

In all three schools, various reasons were suggested for what in each case appeared a voluntary restriction of teacher autonomy. It seemed to us that one important reason for this agreed restriction, this generally accepted view of 'good discipline in our school', was the visible presence of the headteacher. In the three smaller schools, the headteacher moved around the school and was as likely to be out of her/his office as in it. These excursions around the school gave the headteachers daily opportunities to reinforce their policy informally, and to affirm their standards of good discipline. Teacher autonomy may have been restricted, but this restriction was one which teachers saw as positive, setting common boundaries to pupil behaviour, common expectations in terms of teacher standards. Everything interlocked, and relationships too interlocked, a situation which most staff were willing to accept. This restriction did not imply that teachers always behaved in the same ways to achieve good discipline in their classrooms, as Chapters 4 and 5 make clear. However, they were all working towards the same notion of good discipline. The way in which they got there varied according to particular classroom contexts. The benefit of this restriction, which was seen in the schools as affirming the strong interlocking of ideas and attitudes of staff, was that a united discipline policy was highly visible. The cost might be that the very unity of staff views could make change difficult to initiate.

Another benefit which seemed to arise out of restricted autonomy within this interlocking relationship was the concept of communal ownership of the pupils, another idea with important implications for good discipline in the school as a whole.

Whose pupil is it?

When the teachers in Braidburn and Westway talked about good discipline in the school in general, they noted that outside their own classrooms:

> We don't have any qualms about telling them [other teachers' pupils] to behave themselves, there's no grudges held between staff.
>
> (Teacher, Braidburn)

> In other schools in a different atmosphere and maybe a different set up, I think there might be some resentment if you were to do something like that [i.e. intervene to discipline pupils] There is none here.
>
> (Teacher, Westway)

From what the teachers said, it seemed that the pupils were in a sense held in common, a communal responsibility. Again, from what was said, the teachers themselves regarded this as something which could not be taken for granted in all primary schools. Their view was that other teachers in other schools had a concept of 'my class' which would act against efforts to deal effectively with pupil misbehaviour outside the classroom. The communal ownership of pupils was seen as beneficial to good discipline overall, in that teachers felt the pupils saw the teachers as a team, and knew that what they did would not be overlooked by any staff member:

> We are all responsible for other people's children as well.
>
> (Teacher, Westway)

> I suppose some teachers have different levels of expectation [but] probably teachers here do have the same kinds of standards . . . the school's one whole community, you can't just lock yourself away and say, 'this is my class'.
>
> (Teacher, Braidburn)

This sharing also seemed to encourage teachers in feeling positive about their colleagues and their school as well as affirming the worth of good discipline.

> I think it's the nice atmosphere . . . the staff as well, the staff get on very well and they can approach each other without any difficulty. Most of them have a good sense of humour which they share with the children when possible . . . it's good to have that sort of atmosphere among the staff and I think the children see it as well. . .
>
> (Teacher, Braidburn)

> I would say that there is a lot of sharing . . . we discuss the best methods to use . . . in fact it's not just behaviour it's all sorts of other things too . . . We've worked well as a staff and shared a concern for the children.
>
> (Teacher, Westway)

How this change of ownership from 'my class' to 'our pupils' was achieved is not clear, but the role of management in encouraging teachers to share in the life of the school seemed important. We observed communications between headteacher and staff in Braidburn and in Westway which seemed to suggest that headteachers were rewarding the competence of their staff by giving them greater participation in management. For example, the new headteacher at Westway had overturned his predecessor's method of ordering materials whereby the head took sole responsibility. He had given class teachers the responsibility of making up and budgeting their own orders. This may seem rather a small step towards managerial responsibility but, given the history of this school, it was seen by the teachers themselves as an expression of trust and of a policy of sharing. Sharing seemed to be the key to the feeling of a communal responsibility for all pupils, and for the good behaviour of all pupils, not just 'my class'. Did sharing have to be actively pursued as part of the managerial approach?

Although some of the teachers in St Veronica's talked of agreement among colleagues, less mention was made in this school of sharing or of the communal ownership of the pupil. Agreement among teachers seemed to rest on taken-for-granted ideas of what a Catholic education should be. The benefit of this in terms of whole school discipline in the headteacher's view was that:

> I think [it's in] standards overall, any parent coming in would be happy with the standards. The children are very self-contained, they're secure, they're polite, they don't depend on the teachers for sorting things out, they seem to be able to cope with each other.

In the biggest of our primary schools, Oldtown, the communal sharing of pupils seemed less central. Intervention in relation to other teachers' pupils was spoken of more cautiously: '*You do something about it whether the other teacher is offended or not*' [our emphasis]. This compartmentalised rather than communal outlook was something of which management was aware. As the depute headteacher noted: 'I think when I came at first people were a wee bit hesitant about scolding a child in another class in case the teacher was upset or hurt'.

Communal ownership was an idea which was being encouraged in Oldtown in the early stages of the school, at least, and in upper primary, but from what the teachers said, general intervention still did not come readily to staff in this large and rather spread out primary school. The importance of communal ownership of the pupil to achieving acceptable pupil behaviour in the school was not being ignored in Oldtown, but it was something which seemed more difficult to achieve. One reason for this difficulty was the sheer number of pupils; getting to know the children was seen in all the schools as an important factor in both classroom and whole school discipline. The higher number of teachers may also have made managerial attempts at cohesion more difficult. Communal ownership of the pupil could also be affected by the teacher–teacher relationship, which might assist or impede shared responsibility, regardless of what management advocated.

Teacher-teacher relationships

At its most basic, friendly relations between colleagues made teaching more pleasant and alleviated possible stress. As the headteacher at Westway noted: 'They're a friendly staff. If someone is not well, for instance, they'll say, "Nip along to the staff-room and get a cup of tea and I'll take your class".'

Friendly relations between colleagues and being able to enjoy oneself were seen as having indirect or spin-off benefits to the whole school. Friendliness towards colleagues was something which the smaller size of primary schools perhaps made more attainable – or more necessary. To go beyond a surface friendliness seemed to us to move the school towards a team effort and the sharing of pupils. For example, eight of the ten staff in Braidburn talked about support, working together, sharing problems and openly discussing difficulties. An example of this from the field notes concerned pupil behaviour, another concerned sharing ideas about teaching. In the first case a child had taken to running away from school. Discussion in the staff-room focused sympathetically on the child's reason for this, on ways in which the mother could be invited to help without somehow singling out the child too prominently from the rest of the class. Although this child was in an infant class, all staff felt that it was the school's problem, not just the problem of that teacher, and everyone tried to help. In the second case, one of the staff had been on an in-service course which she felt had been very helpful. In telling the others about this course, the teacher found that colleagues from different stages of the school were interested, and the discussion then became one of how a successful idea could be shared or transposed across classes to help pupils with learning difficulties. This discussion ended with material being shared and ideas for progress being identified. Both these examples were small, passing incidents. Nevertheless, the willingness to discuss rather than just let off steam seemed a characteristic of the relationship among teachers in Braidburn. Admitting to problems or to difficulties was not seen as failure; as one teacher observed:

> I think, because of the good relationships, everybody tends to have a sense of humour, so you tend to make a joke about things and I think that helps a lot. When you find other people are having the same problems you'll admit to them and joke about them. I know I've found that it helps you to think, 'I'm not the only one it's happened to'. I think that must be a help.

The same teacher said later of the general standards teachers were expected to keep in the school, 'this is, again, about relationships'. Relationships were more than social politeness. As another teacher summed up, 'We communicate with each other'.

This kind of open discussion and support from teacher to teacher was seen as strengthening discipline in the school. The benefit was 'the happy atmosphere' which allowed a friendly and flexible discipline. In Braidburn, where the teacher–teacher relationship was a direct one, and was based on professional as well as personal contact, a flexible and context-related idea of good discipline seemed to exist. This would accord with the 'family' view of good discipline held in this school, and with the assessment of parents as people rather like the teachers (see Chapter 7).

In St Veronica's, the teacher–teacher relationship was less direct. Here, teachers talked of a common background, a common faith, common expectations of what a Catholic primary school should be like. Friendly relationships did exist between teachers but, given the two separate buildings, direct communication was difficult, as one teacher remarked: 'We're very, very rarely together as a whole staff'. Day-to-day discussion of discipline problems or of discipline policies did not take place. The sharing of problems or the idea of teachers working as a team were not mentioned. We cannot assume such contact was never made, but such relationships were not at the forefront of the teachers' minds when they talked about good discipline in their school. In St Veronica's, the relationship between teachers was not direct, it was one of common reference to an 'outside' standard defined as a Catholic education. It may be considered speculative to suggest that, as the teachers looked to a single, 'correct' definition of how 'our school' should be, they also expected the pupils to accept unquestioningly the teachers' 'correct' definition of good discipline. This speculation accords with the ideas of respect and of the importance of hierarchial authority in St Veronica's, ideas of which the staff approved. One teacher hints at this view as she considers why discipline is good in St Veronica's: 'I found that Catholic schools had better discipline. I don't know why, whether it's because the children are used to going to the church and sitting there and listening . . .'

The obvious benefit of good teacher–teacher relationships is the value attached to joint effort, to the community. This effort has to be a directed one, however. The relationship between management and staff can be used to build on and maximise the benefits of teacher–teacher relationships. Needless to say, there are also obvious costs. If most teachers agree, what becomes of the person with different (but perhaps as valid) views of good discipline? If teachers have strong professional relationships with colleagues, what happens if management is seen as out of step with how discipline is defined in 'our school'? If teacher–teacher relationships are good, and the management–teacher relationship is effective, will complacency set in?

Table 3.1: Benefits and costs: staff relationships

Compartmentalised relationships	Inter-locking relationships
Relationships between teachers and management are hierarchical. Teacher relationships are based on membership of sub-groups (e.g. infant teachers) in the school. Management defines good discipline and supports teachers in dealing with indiscipline.	Relationships between teachers and management are more negotiable. Teacher relationships are based on whole staff concerns and interests. Management and teachers negotiate and agree on definitions of good discipline. Management and teachers give material support in dealing with indiscipline.

HOW DOES THIS AFFECT THE RULES?

Rules are defined by management. Teachers can add to the rules if supported by their sub-group.	Rules are re-negotiated to take account of circumstances. Teachers are expected to have very similar rules.

Benefits

• Teachers are freed from the responsibility and time involved in discussing and defining the rules. • Teachers can expand the rules to the benefit of their own classroom. • There is less likelihood that rules will be misinterpreted by staff and pupils.	• Teachers feel a certain ownership of the rules throughout the school as well as inside the classroom. • Rules can be responsive to the current situation in the school. • The rationale behind rules may be more readily explicable to pupils.

Costs

• Management has to monitor the application of rules, to ensure consistency. • Teachers may feel that rules have been imposed by management.	• Discussion and re-negotiation takes time; some teachers may see this as wasteful. • Disagreement among staff about appropriate rules could be particularly divisive in this interlocking structure.

HOW DOES THIS AFFECT SANCTIONS?

A hierarchy of sanctions is clearly set out by management. How and when these should be applied is made clear.	Sanctions are flexible and teachers are given some latitude in how these should be used.

Benefits

• Teachers may find it easier to be consistent in the application of sanctions. • Teachers feel confident that they will be supported by management. • Automatic sanctions save time for other tasks. • Sanctions are seen as impartial by staff. • Pupils know what will happen throughout the school if rules are broken.	• Teachers are able to judge how to match sanctions to offences and to offenders. • Pupils may see that sanctions are applied after careful consideration on the teacher's part.

Costs

• Teachers may feel restricted, constrained and not fully involved in applying sanctions.	• Time, patience and negotiation are needed to reach a decision on which sanctions are appropriate. • A successful resolution may be dependent on the experience, skill and knowledge of the teacher. • Different standards may be applied by individual teachers; pupils may see this as unfair.

(continued)

Table 3.1   (*continued*)

Compartmentalised relationships	Inter-locking relationships
• It may be difficult for teachers to take individual circumstances into account. • Pupils and teachers could rely too heavily on management as the ultimate sanction. • Pupils may feel that a blanket application of sanctions is unfair.	

HOW DOES THIS AFFECT THE USE OF REWARDS AND PRAISE?

Our data from teachers on rewards and praise were very sparse. We might speculate that the reasons were two-fold:

• teachers did not equate rewards and praise with the discipline system.
• Teachers take the aspect of rewards and praise as an integral part of their teaching and find it difficult to articulate this separately.

We suggest, none the less, that the different management systems might operate in setting down school-wide rewards and praise as they do for defining rules and sanctions.

Conclusion

In this chapter we have discussed the idea that good discipline in the primary school rests on a supportive network of relationships. Two key elements in developing such a network are the relationship between management and teachers, and the relationship among the teachers themselves. Relationships with pupils and with parents are clearly also of importance, and these are discussed elsewhere. In looking at the management–teacher relationship we have emphasised the key role played by the headteacher in dealing with indiscipline and in promoting and maintaining discipline by being visible around the school, in team teaching, in taking over a class from time to time and in setting the overall ethos. We have also noted the key role of the AHT or depute with responsibility for the infant stages in implementing discipline standards. At a general level, the schools operated in very similar ways in promoting and maintaining discipline by emphasising these key roles. More subtle differences were evident in the additional responsibilities given to AHTs, in the amount of autonomy given to classroom teachers, in perceptions of pupils and in relationships among staff. Table 3.1 tries to identify and summarise the benefits and costs of these different approaches. Each approach has strengths and weaknesses. However, it seemed to us that where there were close contacts between the head and staff and among staff, there were greater possibilities of shared ideas and shared responsibilities. Where contact was more distant the teachers had more autonomy. This did not, of course, mean that pupil indiscipline flourished, but it did mean that pupils could meet different standards and expectations in different parts of the school.

We also suspect that a strong teacher–teacher relationship, that is a relationship which moves beyond courtesy and friendliness to professional discussion of discipline and responsibilities, can be fostered by a strong management–teacher relationship. As the headteacher encourages by example and exhorts teachers to maintain the good discipline seen as appropriate in 'our school', some bargain is offered for teacher acceptance of the definition of good discipline and teacher effort to maintain it. One aspect of this bargain is support when things go wrong, when pupils misbehave. At this level, all our schools had such a relationship between management and teachers. Another possible exchange is the sharing of some managerial responsibility; this was found in those schools where there was the strongest shared acceptance of 'good discipline in our school' and the strongest shared view of 'our pupils' rather than 'my class'.

We are not suggesting in this chapter that without a supportive network of management–teacher relationships and teacher–teacher relationships, a primary school will fall to pieces. Nor are we suggesting that these relationships should take the same form in very different schools. We do suggest that where such relationships do exist, the school is the stronger for them and good discipline seems a more attainable objective.

Reviewing staff relationships in your school

Staff relationships in your school may seem quite clear to you. You may be able to use the 'benefits and costs' table to assess ways of maximising the good points of the existing structure, and minimising the costs.

We suggest that you consider this exercise to check your perceptions, or to obtain an insight into the relationships which directly and indirectly affect good discipline in your school.

For unpromoted staff

- Look around the staffroom for a week. Keep notes (discreetly and tactfully):
  - Do people stay in the same groups? Would you say this is a social or a professional common interest, if they do?
  - Is there general discussion of discipline problems? Does this advance beyond letting off steam?
  - Looking at the staff, how would you characterise teacher–teacher relationships? What could be done to build on this?
- Record your contact with the headteacher or head of infants over the week:
  - How often do you see management?

- What sort of contact do you have (i.e. mainly social, or mainly professional, or little contact)?
- Is the contact personal or distant? How do you feel about this? What could you do to improve staff–teacher relationships?

For promoted staff

● Over a period of two weeks, keep notes of:
- Who you see. Do you talk to all staff, some staff (if so, who?) or other senior staff?
- How much time you spend on your staff.
- The quality of this time. Is it social? Professional?
- How you could improve on contact with staff.

References

Bush, T., Glatter, R., Goodey, J. and Riches, C. (eds.) (1980) *Approaches to School Management*, Harper & Row/Open University, London.

Conway, J. (1980) Power and participatory decision-making in selected English schools, in Bush *et al*, op cit.

Gross, N., Giaquinta, J. B. and Bernstein, M. (1971) *Implementing Organisational Innovation: A Sociological Analysis of Planned Educational Change*, Harper & Row, New York.

Nias, J. (1980) Leadership style and job satisfaction in primary schools, in Bush *et al*, op cit.

4
A FRAMEWORK FOR UNDERSTANDING CLASSROOM DISCIPLINE

So far we have been examining whole school discipline policy and practice. We have looked at the differences among schools and summed up the costs and benefits of these different approaches. In this chapter we concentrate on effective classroom discipline and on the similarities among the teachers we studied. These teachers were different from one another in many ways. For example, they taught different ages, had gone to different training colleges and had been teaching for different amounts of time. What they had in common, however, was an approach to promoting classroom discipline. In general terms, this approach consisted of:

- advance planning and preparation to avoid disruption;
- reacting to disruption or to threats of it by using a variety of techniques;
- using their knowledge of individual pupils and the class as a whole to select an appropriate method of discipline;
- being sensitive to a range of influences on their effectiveness, such as time of day, or the subject matter of the lesson.

Before looking in more detail at what the teachers did, we need to stress two points. First, we are reporting teachers' comments about their actions, not observation of their practice. This was because we wanted to get at teachers' own ideas of what was effective, rather than ask them to react to our observation of what seemed to work. Our aim was to try and understand what experienced teachers do routinely and spontaneously in their classrooms by getting them to describe and explain their approach. Second, we are reporting descriptions at a general level in this chapter so that elements of our framework can be explained. Details of the kinds of actions teachers used and the various influences on these actions are in Chapter 5.

How did we choose the teachers and how did we encourage them to talk about their practice?

Choosing the teachers

The research took place in our four case-study primary schools and in each primary we wanted to study two teachers. We believed that this number would permit us to make contrasts and comparisons within each school while not overwhelming us with so much data that thorough analysis would be impossible. How were we to choose the teachers? In our research on second-ary school discipline we had asked pupils to identify teachers who were best at getting the class to work well and to describe what they did; we then used the large number of teachers identified to select the particular teachers to study. We felt that this approach was inappropriate in the primary schools for a number of reasons. First, only the older pupils could be asked for an extended piece of writing and resources did not permit extensive interviews with youn-ger pupils. Second, even if we had been able to collect data from a represent-ative sample of pupils, we thought that comparison among the small number of teaching staff in three of the primary schools to select two teachers to study intensively would be invidious. Third, we assumed we would not be able to use the secondary school criteria of frequency of mention and the range of age groups identifying teachers, to select the particular teachers to study. Primary pupils typically have one class teacher throughout the academic year and would not be in a good position to compare different teachers' approaches to getting the class to work well. Therefore our approach was to explain the purpose of the research to the headteacher and staff in each school and to indicate that we would welcome two volunteers. We also mentioned that we would welcome the opportunity to study teachers of different primary stages. Only one teacher indicated to us that she would be happy to volunteer; and in six cases we approached staff who had indicated that they would be willing but did not directly volunteer. In one further case, a headteacher mentioned that a teacher was being particularly successful with a class generally regarded as difficult and thought that this might be of interest to us. This teacher willingly agreed to participate in the research when approached by us.

Our sample consisted of eight female teachers, with experience ranging from five to eighteen years, from all stages of the school apart from P4. It is clear that our sample of teachers was biased towards those who were willing to take part in classroom research and who taught particular ages of primary pupils. Had we used different criteria for selection, for example, HMI, ad-visers' or headteachers' ratings to identify staff, as well as teachers' willingness to participate, the sample may well have been different.

How did we collect information about teachers' classroom practice?

We describe our research approach in some detail in the Research Appendix (see pages 135–8). Here, we need only make clear that there were two main approaches used to collect information about what teachers did in their classrooms to get the class to work well: observation and interview. We observed each of the eight teachers for part of a day for between seven and twelve days. We usually observed each teacher for segments of one quarter of a day; Oldtown staff preferred half-day segments. We negotiated the particular times and days with the teachers. Observing the teachers at different times of the day, morning or afternoon, for example, gave them the chance to talk about the influence of time and other factors on their approach. For the same reason we tried to observe the pupils doing different kinds of work – number, craft, language, environmental studies – so that teachers, if they wished, could compare and contrast their approaches in potentially different discipline contexts. Observing over a number of days and for quite lengthy sessions gave time for the teachers and pupils to get used to our presence. It also allowed teachers to compare or make references to earlier observed sessions. The observation was unstructured and non-participant. We took no part in the teaching. We noted in general terms what the teacher was doing and what the pupils were doing. The main purpose of the observation was to provide a record as a shared reference point for the teacher and the researcher to discuss.

As near as possible to the observed lesson, sometimes directly afterwards, sometimes in the nearest break or lunchtime, we asked the teacher, 'What did you do to get the class to work well?'. The teachers found this a very difficult question to answer. We were asking them to make explicit their routine, taken-for-granted behaviour in their classrooms. We had many requests to suggest to the teachers what *we* thought they had done to get the class to work well, but the whole point of our approach was to elicit from teachers their own constructs of what they did. This meant that initial interviews were often very brief, perhaps five minutes or so, as teachers said all they had to say about their practice. Our only probes were, 'Can you tell me a bit more about that?' and 'Why did you do that?' and 'Was that the same as in lesson such and such?' However, as time went on, the teachers gradually had more to say, perhaps because they knew they were going to be talking about their actions and so became more conscious of them. It may be, of course, that they became more expert at providing 'rationalisations' rather than 'true explanations' of their practice. Our approach to collecting and analysing the information about teachers' classroom practice closely mirrors that of Brown and McIntyre (1988) in their study of teachers' professional craft knowledge, and we say more about the approach in the appendix.

Making sense of effective classroom discipline

The remainder of this chapter sets out the framework we have derived from analysing teachers' descriptions and explanations of what they do to get their classes to work well. The framework is grounded in teachers' actual practice, not in what they think they ought to do or what they would do in ideal circumstances. In analysing teachers' interviews we discounted all general statements such as 'Typically I would' or 'Normally I do' if these did not refer to the lesson in hand. We wanted to develop an understanding of what teachers did, not what they should do. Accordingly, in analysing their interviews, a teacher action was something the teacher said she did in the observed lesson, such as, 'I asked them to quieten down'.

An interesting feature of the primary teachers' discourse is that sometimes the infant staff, in particular, talked about 'we' rather than 'I'. For example, a P2 teacher, describing a part of her lesson, said: 'We spent the first portion of the afternoon listening to the tape, stopping it, discussing it, taking part'. And another teacher from a different school reported: 'We got up and moved over to the blackboard'. Similarly, in a third school, a teacher talking about letter recognition said: 'We did that with the alphabet . . . turning it from purely doing it on the blackboard to this game'. In feeding back our analysis of their classroom actions to the teachers we asked them specifically to comment on this and whether it was appropriate to interpret this kind of discourse as being about the actions they employed as individuals. The teachers who tended to talk in these terms indicated that in talking about 'we' they meant 'I'. It is interesting to speculate that the use of the term 'we' indicates a strong sense of identification with the pupils as a class, a group involved together in learning and in developing as social beings.

The teachers involved in the research worked in four different schools teaching pupils at a variety of ages and stages and had themselves undergone pre-service training at different institutions. In addition, they varied in their career patterns, some having worked in a number of different schools and others having experience in only one or two schools. To develop a framework which helped understanding of how teachers went about promoting and maintaining classroom discipline meant that the framework had to be at a general level. Chapter 5 fleshes out the framework by giving examples of the ways in which the teachers acted and the kinds of influences which they saw as impinging upon their actions. This chapter sets out the elements which make up the framework of how teachers get their classes to work well. These are as follows:

- actions which are proactive and actions which are reactive;
- a sign or signs to provoke reactions;
- two kinds of teachers' judgements – whether to act and how to act;
- a range of conditions affecting teachers' actions;
- a range of goals influencing teachers' actions.

We describe each of these elements in more detail below.

The importance of planning

When our eight teachers talked about what they had done to get their class to work well, it soon became apparent that they did some things in advance of the pupils appearing in their classrooms. For example, they would make sure they were in the classroom before the pupils arrived, or they would have equipment and materials laid out ready for a particular piece of work. These kinds of statements we called 'proactive' because they were taken in advance of any sign that the class was not working well. However, these proactive approaches did not just apply to the teachers' physical presence in the classroom or to laying out materials. The teachers also talked about their lesson planning; for instance, making connections with previous work done by the pupils, thinking through in advance how to explain a difficult topic or concept and thinking about what kinds of activities would interest their pupils. The following are two examples of what we saw as proactive approaches to maintaining classroom discipline. In the first, a P7 teacher is talking about using the computer and she remarks concisely: 'I was very well prepared, I had looked at my computer program . . . I knew what it involved'. In the second, a P2 teacher describes her approach to planning a range of activities for several groups of children, giving an idea of the organisational skills and forward planning she considers necessary to avoid disruption:

Researcher: What was it, do you think, that you did to make the class work well?
Teacher: Well, the main thing, I think, was preparation on my part. I mean I have to be prepared . . . I have to have the tracing paper out and ready in the pile, all the maths books have to be ready . . . and the same with [the group] who are going to be working with the money . . . they were going to need the [real] money and at 9 o'clock before they started I just got them to line up and someone from one of the other groups gave out the money that they needed which they then put on their table . . . they were all ready to start . . . And I also had the group with the cubes all ready to start . . . I find that it works [this way] rather than when pupils moved out. They would all be trying to find cubes to take to their tables and the people who needed money would all be looking for money . . . I find if I don't give [materials] out initially, then they all come and mill around and they'll interrupt the group that you're teaching.

Being proactive, then, means that teachers prepare things in advance, they do not wait for something to happen to prevent the class from working well before taking action. Interestingly enough, the notion of being proactive as an aid to effective discipline has been used by other writers. In the USA, Kounin (1970), for example, using a different research technique, found that what distinguished effective classroom managers was not their ability to deal with disruptions once they arose but their ability to prevent disruption in the first place. Similarly, Wragg and Wood (1984) in this country found that effective classroom managers are those who reduce opportunities for disruption and develop positive relationships with pupils. There are certainly many excellent texts on classroom management, usually aimed at the novice teacher, which emphasise the need for careful preparation, planning and organisation, and our teachers conformed to this pattern. They talked more about being proactive, avoiding opportunities for disruption, than about reacting to trouble.

Reacting to disruption

Reactive approaches are those actions which are triggered by a sign or signs that all is not well. Here the teacher is responding to a cue that individual pupils, or groups, or the class as a whole are not working well. Some examples illustrate this kind of action.

> Tony was beginning to fidget [while watching a TV broadcast of 'Storytime']. I had to turn to look at him.

> Michelle [has been] a wee bit chatty lately . . . Now I decided to put her outside . . . She just wasn't going to take a telling this morning, for some reason . . . I mean every time I looked round she was running about. . . .I spoke to her outside and said to her . . . 'Really, this sort of behaviour is not on'.

> He was actually throwing things about in the Wendy House . . . I sent him back through into the classroom area.

Some signs indicated that the class was working well and teachers talked about positive steps they took in response to good work or behaviour as reinforcement. Praise and rewards did not feature strongly in either teacher or pupil data from the schools, with the notable exception of Westway, but it did occur. For example, in St Veronica's a teacher mentioned: 'Rosalind . . . was having great problems with the number line and the adding . . . I feel she can do it but her confidence isn't there. So I thought if I . . . just give her a wee pat, you know [and say] "That's great", that [instils] a bit of confidence'. The teacher's reaction to Rosalind's difficulty with numbers was to encourage her and praise her. Most of the admittedly sparse data we have on rewards and praise concerns effort at work rather than at behaving well. In part this may be a result of the question we asked, 'What did you do to get the class to work well?' – but it is noteworthy that bad behaviour almost always provokes a reaction, a sanction or punishment. Good behaviour is rarely rewarded or reinforced.

So far we have described one element in our framework, that of teachers' actions, and we have tried to show that there are two kinds of actions: those which are proactive, taken before there is any indication that the class is not working well and those which are reactions to potential disruption. We have stressed that these ideas have been found by other researchers and that a characteristic of being effective in getting the class to work well is to use proactive approaches as well as reactive ones. There are many influences on the teacher's judgement about whether to take action and, if so, what action to take. It is to these that we now turn. These influences affect both proactive and reactive approaches.

Influences on teachers' actions

Conditions

The context in which teaching is carried out has a profound effect on what teachers do and on what they count as getting the class to work well. What works in one lesson for one teacher with a particular group of pupils will not necessarily work for the same teacher with the same group of pupils in a different lesson, far less for a range of teachers and pupils. One only has to think of the difference between teaching mid-morning on a Monday and last thing on a Friday afternoon to see the force of this point. Many writers have pointed out the context specific nature of discipline and how far we are from being able to satisfy beginning teachers' demands for recipe knowledge about how to achieve effective discipline in all circumstances. In analysing our teachers' comments, we were struck by their references to the context in which they were teaching as affecting their actions, and it is this context which we have called 'conditions'. We have classified conditions into a number of categories which we discuss at greater length in Chapter 5. For the moment we wish to get across the idea that conditions influence teachers' actions and are an important element in our framework. We include here a small number of examples and try to show how they impinge on teachers' actions.

One of the most frequently mentioned conditions mentioned by our eight teachers was what we have called 'knowledge of the pupil' – for instance, knowledge about the pupil's home background, his or her behaviour in previous years in the school or particular abilities. Teachers often cited what they knew about a particular pupil as influencing their decision about whether to act and what action to take. We are not suggesting that such knowledge was necessarily accurate or complete; merely that what teachers believe they know about pupils influences their actions.

In the following example the teacher explains her action, calling the pupil out to her desk, in terms of her knowledge of the pupil: 'I called him out to see what he had done. He has difficulty in concentrating'.

As we shall see in Chapter 5, references to knowledge of the individual pupil was one of the most frequently mentioned influences, or conditions, affecting teachers' actions. Almost as frequent were references to knowledge of the class as a whole, as how it would be likely to respond in various situations. In the following extract the teacher explains her finely balanced interest in a pupil's holiday in terms of her knowledge of the class being jealous at the amount of attention being given to one pupil:

> And for the child who had been on holiday, I made sure I was aware she'd been on holiday and took an interest in where she'd been but not too much, otherwise the others might have been a bit jealous or felt a bit peeved about it. So I made sure that she knew I knew she'd been away and she was back.

Similarly, there were many references to groups of pupils in the class in terms of their abilities, motivation and general attitude. The following is a typical example: 'It was just a case of going round observing and helping as necessary. There wasn't really a group that needed me with them to direct that group. They were all fairly sure of what they were doing'. And again: 'I did a wee bit of back-pedalling [over the content] with him but there's not much point in speaking to Graham alone, the rest of the group are going to be like that'.

In all, teacher references to knowledge of individuals, groups or the class as a whole far outweighed any other condition influencing their actions and we shall return later to the implications of this. For the moment, however, our concern is with exemplifying what we mean by a condition influencing actions, and we offer one more example, that of time. The teachers talked about the time of the week, the time of day, the time of year and about the amount of time they preferred to spend on particular classroom activities as an influence on their actions.

> I didn't ask them to write straight away . . . Monday morning's a tricky morning for everyone.

> I sent Tom to search for the others as it was now the end of the day [and there was] not much time left.

> I said today they could choose anything apart from the jigsaws or boxes . . . I said they could have the lego. It was the last week of term.

Teachers seldom mentioned only one condition related to any particular action. It was typical for two or three conditions to be referred to as bearing upon actions. Thus, Tom was selected to search for the others, in the example above, because the teacher knew he had finished his work and believed he was a sensible boy who could be trusted with the task. The task itself, the searching for the other pupils, was triggered by the time of day. Conditions, however, are not the only influence on teachers' actions. The final element in our framework is that of goals and we now describe what these are and how they influence actions.

Goals

In any lesson a teacher has a goal or, more usually, a number of goals. There are things which the teacher hopes will be achieved during the course of the lesson or as the end result of the lesson. The teacher can have goals for the class as a whole, for example, that it completes a project by Christmas, and goals for a particular pupil, for example, that she contributes to a group or class discussion. We discuss in more detail in Chapter 5 the kinds of goals which teachers have. Here we want to suggest that teachers' goals influence the actions they take in order to get the class to work well. For example, in the following extract the teacher's goal is to get the pupils to produce models and machines for later display:

> I'd just told them where to go and get the materials because they're still not familiar with where everything is kept . . . So once these have been made, perhaps during this week some time, we will put up a display [indicating] 'This is so and so's machine used for [such and such]'.

Similarly in talking about placing two boys on either side of her, the teacher below offers an explanation in terms of getting them to do some work, her goal for these two pupils in maths:

> As you know I've got to keep an eye on Robert and Paul – you must know them by this time! I've started a system to get them to do their SPMG work by having them actually sit one on either side of me at the table. Now, I'm dealing with the two of them and the reading group round about because if I don't do that they will do nothing.

Goals can be in conflict and can assume different orders of priority. The following teacher is describing sorting out her class into groups. She has goals of wanting children to get through work which is most appropriate for them. She is also anxious not to label children and demotivate one child in particular by moving him to less demanding work. She also wishes groups to promote personal and social development. So her perception of her pupils' abilities is not the only criterion on which groups are formed:

> I let the groups form naturally, form themselves. I do use [information from other staff] . . . but I see for myself and I check this is true . . . Part of my discipline is knowing the ones who can do the whole exercise and the ones that can't do it. I keep an eye on it. . . . So at present I'm sorting out those who will benefit from a formal project and, of course, there are always those in the middle that don't quite fit any slot. . . . I've already found one who's very weak and he knows. . . . That is a problem, not to upset that child to the extent that he's . . . not going to feel completely depressed or hopeless. . . . It's a big problem. And he's going to feel it if he's moved down a group and given work which he can perhaps cope with. He can't cope with the idea [of not being in group 1].

This extract illustrates the conflicting goals of maintaining a child's confidence and motivation on the one hand and using ability groups for maths work to enable each child to make progress through the work. A further complication was that as the groups formed themselves in friendship groups, promoting goals of group cohesion and solidarity, these did not necessarily correspond with ability groups. This teacher resolved these conflicting goals through her approach to classroom organisation. Group work was not concerned with the sharing of common problems. Rather each child tended to work individually. Each child knew which group he or she belonged to and the teacher would call, for example, 'Group 1 maths please come to this table!'. The children would get up from their mixed ability groups around the classroom and congregate at the designated table.

This example demonstrates the complexity of teacher decision-making. The teacher's decisions on the purposes of group work and on the composition of groups were influenced by a range of things:

- her goal that group work shouuld promote learning about the academic curriculum
- her goal that group work should encourage pupils' social skills
- her knowledge of her pupils in terms of mathematical ability, motivation and emotional development (condition)
- her knowledge of the mathematics syllabus (condition)

This interplay of goals and conditions led to the complex arrangements for group work described above.

The interplay of goals, conditions and actions

The extract from the teacher's interview immediately above illustrates how a condition – knowledge of the pupils' abilities – influenced her goals and hence her actions. Her belief and knowledge about her pupils' abilities helped her to 'sort out those who would benefit from a formal project' and we can infer from what she says about the boy who is weak that she has different cognitive goals for him than for those pupils who are 'stronger' intellectually. She is in something of a dilemma about what action to take ('It's a big problem') because moving the boy to a less intellectually demanding maths group would realise, she believes, her cognitive goals for the boy only if she can do so in such a way to avoid 'demoralising and upsetting him'. It is clear, then, that a condition such as knowledge of the pupil can affect the selection of particular goals and perhaps their order of priority. So an infant teacher may prioritise particular social training goals, given what she believes she knows about the likely characteristics of four- and five-year-olds. Similarly, the cognitive goals for five year olds will not be the same as those for ten-year-olds.

In our framework, the overarching goal which we suggested to teachers was that of getting the class to work well. However, as can be seen from the small number of examples already given, teachers talked to us about a number of other goals which they had and sometimes explicitly linked these to the perceived context in which they were working. In the diagram (Figure 4.1) setting out our framework there is, therefore, an arrow linking goals and conditions. It is tempting to speculate that experienced teachers are expert at matching goals and conditions; in other words, that they know what are appropriate and realistic goals for a given set of conditions. It seems likely that they have a repertoire of goals which they can pull out as appropriate to particular conditions operating in their classrooms. It also seems likely that when goals and conditions 'match' the opportunities for disruption are reduced – although, of course, the actions which the teacher takes also affect the occurrence or not of disruption. Correspondingly, when goals and conditions are out of kilter, opportunities for disruption are likely to be increased. There are many questions posed by our information from teachers about what they do to get the class to work well. Not least among these questions is how teachers build up a repertoire of actions and goals and how they come to recognise their appropriateness in particular sets of circumstances. We can offer some limited and speculative answers to these questions, generated from our eight teachers. However, before we do so let us sum up the elements of the framework which describes what teachers do to get their classes to work well. These are:

- that teachers use proactive and reactive approaches;
- that reactions are provoked by signs (a particular class of conditions);
- that a range of conditions impinge on teachers' decisions about whether to act and how to act;
- that a range of goals influence actions and that goals can be in conflict;
- that conditions affect the selection and order of priority of goals;

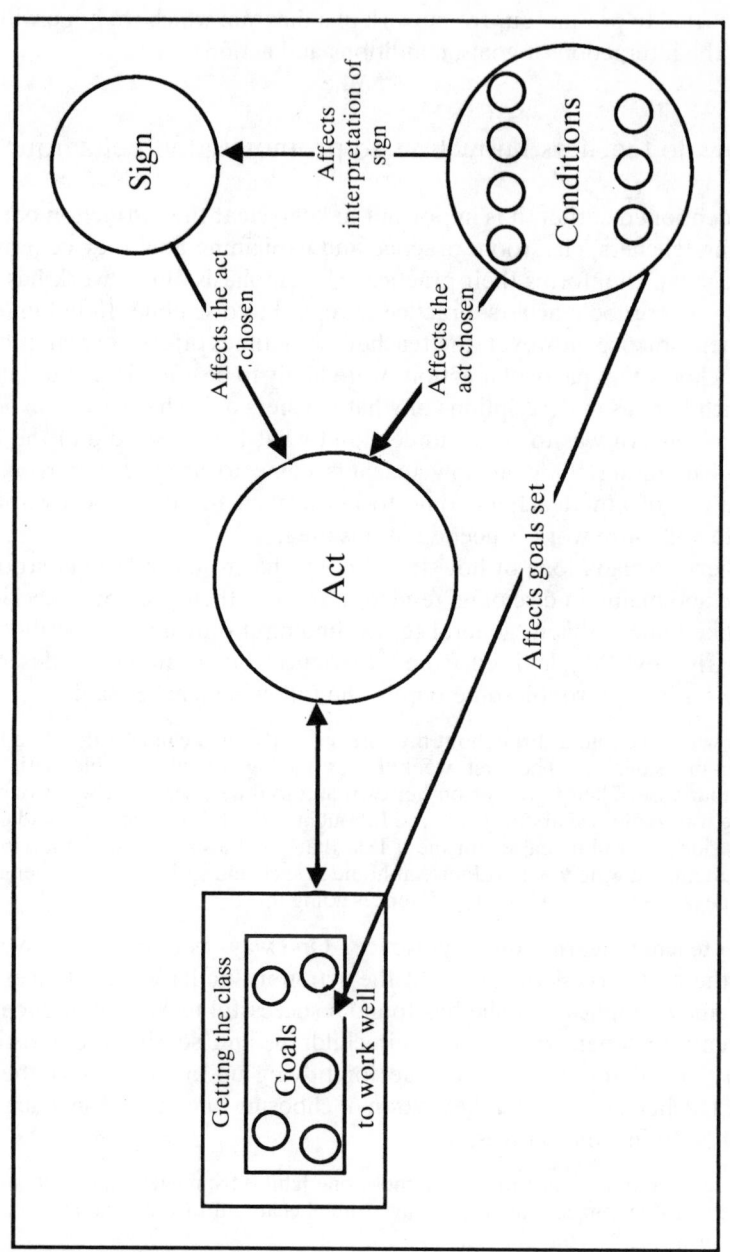

Figure 4.1   How do teachers talk about getting the class to work well?

- that conditions affect the achievement of goals.

We have tried to present our framework in a diagram which we hope will help to show the interaction of goals, conditions and actions.

How do teachers know how to promote good behaviour?

As we mentioned earlier, it is important to keep clear the distinction between describing teachers' classroom practice and explaining how they acquire the knowledge which informs their practice. The emphasis of our work has been in trying to describe teachers' practice in regard to discipline. In talking to us about their practice, however, the teachers sometimes offered explanations of how they knew that particular actions were likely to be effective. Our data are not as rich here as in descriptions of what teachers did. This is to be expected since our concern was to try to understand what teachers did and the influences on it, rather than on how teachers come to acquire expertise. The explanations of how teachers come to know what to do are necessarily incomplete and more work is needed in this area.

Teachers' explanations of how they know what to do in the classroom to promote and maintain discipline tended to refer to their previous experience. They talked about this in general terms, finding it difficult to describe more particularly how they learned from experience. For example, in describing how she reacted to troublesome pupils, the following teacher said:

> That's what I've found throughout my career . . . I've had children that I've had to get on my side. . . . The first week I was having terrible trouble with Mary, behaviour-wise. Then I got her on her own and told her, her work was wonderful. . . .She was so pleased about this . . . so I thought, 'Right, I'll get in there and get her on my side, life will be easier for me if I do that'. . . .I also find that with parents. I say to them, 'How do you find James at home at such and such?' . . . and then they'll start speaking. [I try to avoid] the defences going up.

How do teachers learn from experience? One way, as indicated above, was that of the past success or failure of the action in similar circumstances. The teacher above implies that she has found a successful technique in encouraging parents to 'open up' about their children, and so she keeps using it. Similarly, in talking about a routine for tidying up at the end of the day, another teacher explains that her action of choosing one pupil from each table is based on trying alternatives:

> It just saves a lot of confusion. . . . I chose one [child] from each table instead of all children putting things away. It also saves time because if I were to go round it takes a lot longer.

Teachers also talked of their beliefs about teaching as an explanation for taking particular actions to get the class to work well. These were many and varied. Infant teachers commented, for example, on the need to set aside time early on to teach tying of shoelaces and getting changed for gym. Others tended to talk more generally; the following extracts illustrate the range of beliefs mentioned:

> I can't, as a teacher, sit [at the desk] with a pile of corrections. Teaching is being involved with the children. You must go round [and look at and talk about] their work.

> I feel [building up] a good relationship with the parents is essential. . . .I think it's important that [the children] talk about the teacher as a person and that the parent gets to know what that person is like.

> I think it's a basic human right to be sent out to school when they're their age, clean and fresh. I think you start at a great disadvantage to come into school dirty, with sleep in your eyes, your hair not brushed. . . .By the age of children in my class [eight or nine years old] I do try to encourage them to make sure their faces, their hands, their feet, are clean. . . . It is part of the social training we have to do – it's a social grace.

There were some references, too, to school regional or national guidelines as explanations for actions, and to initial training, but these were very sparse.

How can experienced teachers help new teachers?

This chapter has tried to provide a framework for understanding how teachers talk about getting the class to work well; it has three main elements: actions; goals; and conditions. It is essentially simple and in many ways it would be surprising if it were more elaborate if it is an accurate representation of the concepts which teachers operationalise in getting the class to work well. The wide-ranging nature of the teacher's job and the unpredictability of the whole business of teaching would suggest that a complicated framework would not be workable in the day-to-day reality of classrooms. We have tried to show that the apparent simplicity of the framework camouflages the complexity of the decision-making in which teachers engage as they promote and maintain effective discipline. We have given brief examples of the wide range of conditions that impinge upon teachers' actions. We have given examples, too, of the different kinds of goals which teachers have and which may be in conflict. Finally, we have classified teachers' actions as proactive or reactive.

For the moment, it may be asked, 'How can we use this framework?' It seems to us that its main usefulness could be in the training of beginning teachers and in the professional development of probationers. However, we should stress that we are offering suggestions. We have not undertaken research on how beginning teachers might learn from experienced teachers and in what follows we have made assumptions about the benefits of observing experienced teachers at work in the classroom and of discussions between experienced teachers and beginning teachers. We do not know how experienced teachers acquired their expertise and so it is something of a leap in the dark to suggest ways in which novice teachers could learn. With that caveat in mind we offer three ways of using our framework.

Helping beginning teachers to analyse classroom practice

Beginning teachers are presented with marvellous opportunities to observe other teachers at work. These opportunities rapidly disappear once pre-service days are over and so it is important that the maximum benefit is achieved from classroom observation. There have been many books designed to help students observe classrooms. However, these tend to concentrate on techniques of observation or on particular techniques of classroom control. They have not tended to provide an overall conceptualisation of what teachers are doing as they go about getting the class to work well. We see our framework as being a potentially useful adjunct to the classroom observation texts already available in providing such a conceptualisation. For example, groups of students studying a video of experienced teachers at work could be alert for the distinction between proactive and reactive approaches; they could be asked to note the explicit conditions operating in the classroom, such as numbers of pupils, seating arrangements, subject matter of the lesson and so on. However, they could also discuss any clues about implicit conditions from comments made by the teacher and pupils. There might be clues about the previous behaviour of the pupils, for instance, or the teacher's knowledge about a particular pupil.

Of course, there are severe limitations to the amount of useful information to be derived from classroom observation only. Talking to teachers about what they are doing and why is an essential part of gaining access to experienced teachers' knowledge. Some recent research has shown the extremely limited time spent in conversation between student teachers and experienced teachers when on school placement (McNab and Kennedy, 1989). Clearly, structures need to be provided to ensure that there is time for both parties to discuss specific lessons. How can we ensure that if time is provided for such discussion it is rewarding for all concerned? We suggest that a version of our approach to collecting data, namely asking teachers in an open-ended way what they had done to get the class to work well, may be a fruitful way of beginning teachers getting access to experienced teachers' craft knowledge. Our experience was that teachers gradually had more to say about their practice as the research progressed. It may be that one way of increasing the value of conversations between experienced and beginning teachers is to use this kind of approach. Experiments in this have already been tried in Oxford and Glasgow which have provided some encouraging results (see Brown *et al.*, 1989). Much work remains to be done here not only in providing the right kinds of structures to enable such conversations to take place but, more fundamentally, in teachers becoming accustomed to talking about the nature of their expertise. One of the most important elements in generating such talk is locating discussion in a particular lesson observed by the student. In this way teachers are encouraged to talk about what they did rather than what they would like to have done. Clearly, it is also vital that students make their approaches in a friendly and non-judgemental way if they are to encourage staff to talk freely and frankly.

Helping beginning teachers to reflect upon their practice

Many initial teacher training courses aim to encourage their students to reflect systematically on their classroom experience. Our framework provides one kind of structure to that systematic reflection. Students could ask themselves if they were proactive, for example, and if they became progressively more proactive during their school practice. Similarly, they could ask themselves if their goals and the planning to achieve those goals took sufficient account of the conditions operating in their classrooms. In essence, our framework provides one way of understanding the nature of classroom discipline. It is saying to new teachers that they do not have to rely on trial and error, or to see classroom events as 'one damn thing after another'. There is a pattern to the complex series of classroom events and in understanding that pattern they improve their ability to plan to get the class to work well. Contexts for such student reflection need not always be private. There might be scope to use the framework in the debriefing that takes place with fellow students after micro-teaching, for example. Alternatively, students could work in pairs in planning and analysing lesson plans before they go out on teaching practice.

Helping beginning teachers to develop their lesson planning

Research has shown that beginning teachers rely much more heavily on formal lesson plans than experienced teachers. The important point to make here concerns the formality of lesson planning by experienced teachers on the one hand and beginning teachers on the other. Many experienced teachers do not plan their lesson by writing out detailed aims and objectives, the time allocation of particular parts of the lesson, the key questions to be used, and the kinds of actions they propose to adopt – the items typically contained in a student teacher's lesson plan. However, our data from experienced teachers reveal that sophisticated planning goes on in their heads and suggest that, as teachers gain experience, they build up repertoires of actions and goals and become expert at recognising when certain conditions call for their use. The data suggest that experienced teachers not only have a repertoire on which to plan but also use the repertoire to adapt plans if things are not going well.

Our framework suggests a particular kind of structure for the lesson plans of beginning teachers. It points up the need for students to be clear about the goals of their lessons and this will come as no surprise to those involved in teacher training. This is already a feature of many colleges' pre-service courses. Our identification of a relationship between goals and conditions suggests that students need to be able to justify their goals in the light of the prevailing conditions, such as the age range of the pupils; the time of day of the lesson, the previous work done by the pupils, and their knowledge of the pupils. These are only a few of the conditions that impinge on experienced teachers' planning, as we shall see in Chapter 5. It would be unrealistic to expect new teachers to be able to make good judgements about the conditions affecting their teaching and so the regular class teacher becomes an important source of help. We see possibilities of our framework being used to develop a checklist of conditions which beginning teachers could use in seeking advice from experienced teachers about the appropriateness of particular goals.

Our simple framework of the key concepts which teachers use in getting the class to work well distinguishes proactive and reactive approaches to maintaining discipline. As we mentioned at the beginning of this chapter, many studies have shown that effective classroom discipline arises from proactive planning. In other words, experienced teachers prevent opportunities for disruption arising through their planning. They do not wait for trouble to occur. This points to the need for beginning teachers to be as proactive as possible in their planning, not only because this is what experienced teachers do, but also because new teachers do not have the repertoires of actions which experienced teachers have to call on and if disruption does occur they will not have the same resources to deal with it. New teachers, therefore, need to be thoroughly briefed about the school and subject department procedures for dealing with disruption, the sanctions which are available and so on. Again, this will not come as news to those involved in teacher training. What may be news is the need to make explicit the rationale for all this information. This is not to make beginning teachers feel even more insecure than they do already. Rather it is to convey an understanding of the differences between experienced and beginning teachers in one area of classroom practice; to be seen to be providing practical support for new teachers and to make clear that experienced teachers are there to help. If both parties can conceptualise what it is they are doing in terms of the framework we have suggested, we hope they will be provided with a practical approach to making sense of one aspect of teaching – classroom discipline. Crucially, we hope they will begin to see that the framework is a basis for reflecting on their practice and for helping their professional development as teachers.

References

Brown, S. and McIntyre, D. (1988) The professional craft knowledge of teachers, in W. A. Gatherer (ed.) *The Quality of Teaching. A Special Issue of Scottish Educational Review*, pp. 39–47.

Brown, S. and McIntyre, D. (1989) *Making Sense of Teaching*, Scottish Council for Research in Education, Edinburgh.

Brown, S., McIntyre, D., Haggar, H. and McAlpine, A. (1989) *Student Teachers Learning from Experienced Teachers*, Scottish Council for Research in Education, Edinburgh.

Bull, S. and Solity, J. E. (1987) *Classroom Management: Principles to Practice*, Croom Helm, Beckenham.

Calderhead, J. (1979) Teachers' classroom decision-making: its relationship to teachers' perceptions of pupils and to classroom interaction. Unpublished Ph.D. thesis. University of Stirling.

Calderhead, J. (1984) *Teachers' Classroom Decision-Making*, Holt, Rinehart & Winston, London.

Calderhead, J. (ed.) (1988) *Teachers' Professional Knowledge*, Falmer Press, Lewes.

Clark, C. M. and Yinger, R. J. (1987) Teaching planning, in J. Calderhead (ed.) *Exploring Teachers' Thinking*, Cassell, London.

Denscombe, M. (1985) *Classroom Control: A Sociological Perspective*, Allen & Unwin, London.

Francis, P. (1975) *Beyond Control? A Study of Discipline in the Comprehensive School*, Unwin Educational Books, London.

Galloway, D. (1982) Learning from experience: a course for advisory teachers, *British Journal of In-service Education*, 8, 3, pp. 177–80.

Good, T. L. and Brophy, J. C. (1978) *Looking in Classrooms*, Harper & Row, London.

Kounin, J. (1970) *Discipline and Group Management in Classrooms*, Holt, Rinehart & Winston, New York.

Kyriacou, C. (1986) *Effective Teaching in Schools*, Basil Blackwell, Oxford.

McNab, D. and Kennedy, M. (1989) *Student Teacher Talk: An Empirical Study of PGCE Students in Schools*, Northern College, Aberdeen.

Reynolds, D. (1985) *Studying School Effectiveness*, Falmer Press, Lewes.

Robertson, J. (1981) *Effective Classroom Control*, Hodder & Stoughton, London.

Schulman, L. S. (1986) Those who understand: knowledge growth in teaching, *Educational Researcher*, February 4–14.

Schwab, J. (1971) The practical: arts of eclectic, *School Review*, 79, 4.

Walker, R. and Adelman, C. (1987) *A Guide to Classroom Observation*, Methuen, London.

Wilson, S. M., Schulman, L. S. and Richert, A. E. (1987) 150 different ways of knowing: representations of knowledge in teaching, in J. Calderhead (ed.) *Exploring Teachers' Thinking*, Cassell, London.

Wragg, E. C. (1981) *Class Management and Control*, Macmillan, London.

Wragg, E. C. and Wood E. K. (1984) Teachers' first encounters with their classes in E. C. Wragg (ed.) *Classroom Teaching Skills*, Croom Helm, Beckenham.

5
PROMOTING EFFECTIVE CLASSROOM DISCIPLINE

In this chapter we examine teachers' actions and the influences on their actions in some detail. Tables describing these, and the frequency with which teachers talked about them, illustrate the relative importance of certain actions, conditions or goals for the eight teachers as a whole and show:

- the importance of setting a clear framework for pupils by giving instructions and organising work so as to minimise opportunities for disruption;
- the high number of references to preparation and planning, class organisation and explaining and helping children who were 'stuck';
- that teachers need to be constantly on their toes for signs of bad behaviour and for nipping it in the bud.

The tables necessarily underplay any differences among the four schools. Of course, individual teachers differ in the actions they take, the conditions they recognise as salient and in their prioritisation of goals. Our point here is that, in the context of a particular school, a key idea such as the school's view of its pupils might influence the teacher's selection of a particular action, if conditions and goals allow for a degree of choice. Westway teachers may talk differently from Oldtown teachers about their classrooms, for instance. However, our approach has been to concentrate on the similarities across the eight teachers as a group, rather than upon school differences.

What do teachers do to get their classes to work well?

It will be remembered that at the end of every lesson we observed with our eight teachers we asked the question, 'What did you do to get the class to work well?' For the teachers' responses to count as valid, two broad criteria had to be met.

- The statement had to refer to something that the teachers had done in the observed lesson. Statements such as, 'Typically I would do such and such, but I didn't do that today,' were discounted.

- The teachers had to generate their own ideas about what they had done. Any suggestion that the researchers might have been leading the teachers to talk about particular actions meant that we discounted these statements. So, for example, an exchange such as a researcher saying, 'I noticed you did such and such', and the teacher then responding to that, was discounted.

Using these criteria we were able to count 198 statements about effective actions taken by the teachers. We have grouped these statements into fifteen categories and these are given in Table 5.1. The labels given to the categories have been devised by us. However, under each category we give some examples of the statements made by the teachers to give an idea of the kinds of things they said about their classroom practice. We also indicate the number of references made to particular actions.

There are a number of points to make about this table. The first concerns the dominance of the category of giving instructions and organising work. Our teachers' discourse was dominated by the need to plan to get the class to work well and to minimise opportunities for disruption by ensuring that the pupils knew what they had to do, knew where to find materials and knew which group they belonged to. Just how dominant were these proactive approaches? After all, giving instructions could be reactive, a response to a lot of children asking where to find materials, or proactive. An analysis of statements revealed that almost 80 per cent of actions were proactive in that the teachers did not indicate that they were responding to signs of disruption. Again, we must be cautious about claiming too much for this figure as our approach to getting teachers to talk about their practice may have encouraged them to focus on their planning and preparation. Had we asked them how they responded to pupil misbehaviour we would, no doubt, have seen different patterns of actions.

The second point to make about the table follows from the first. The number of comments relating to the use of sanctions is very small, only 3 per cent, and these, indeed, came from only one school. This suggests that the amount of serious rule-breaking was insignificant and that the teachers relied on a range of other actions to avoid trouble arising or to defuse trouble in the making. There were, similarly, few references to using warnings and verbal rebukes. It is perhaps worth adding here that the sparing use of sanctions was borne out by our own classroom observations. There were very few instances of a child being punished in our observed lessons by, for instance, being sent to the headteacher or being banned from an activity. The child mucking about in the Wendy House was the most obvious case of disruption and the teacher discussed this subsequently in interview. Of course, as many writers have pointed out, there is a hierarchy of sanctions which teachers can employ, ranging from a raised eyebrow and standing beside a pupil to the issuing of punishment exercises and detention. Among our teachers the use of sanctions further up the hierarchy in terms of seriousness was conspicuous by its

Table 5.1: Teachers' actions to get the class to work well

Category	Examples of teachers' statements	N = 198	%	Category	Examples of teachers' statements	N = 198	%
Gives instructions/ organises work	I just told them where to go and get the materials. I said that everyone had to get on with what they'd been working on.	88	44	Gives warnings	I turned to Rachel and gave her a warning look. I mentioned that about Lynne's holiday treat as a warning.	5	3
Explains/helps	I showed them what to do and told them the next step. We (I) talked . . . We (I) introduced the strong man in this shape of the letter.	26	13	Personal contact (Refers to actions designed to promote positive pupil–teacher relationships)	I had to take an interest in the child who had been on holiday. (In response to a personal question about the teacher) I kind of went back to her and said, 'Well, I don't think (I am related to Y) but I'll ask.	5	3
Observes/positions (Refers to use of teacher position in the classroom to observe the children/or make her presence felt)	I sat among them. I sat at one of the middle tables and asked the children to come out and show me what they had done so far. I was just watching them really.	21	10	Allows infringement of rules	I let them go and play with the toys (because he'd concentrated for as long as he could?)	4	2
Verbal rebukes	I gave him a row. I had a word with them about that.	10	5	Asks questions	I said, 'Who's singing? Was that Mary?' I asked them if Alastair had been involved.	4	2

(continued)

Table 5.1 (*continued*)

Category		Examples		
Rewards/enjoyment/ praise	8	I said, 'Yes, good. That's a good word'. I told the ones (who'd done) the story . . . that they'd done a good job.		
Uses humour	4	I went out of my way this morning to have a joke. I picked up her arm (pretending that I thought she'd fainted).	2	1
Prepares/plans	7	I worked out how much was needed for everyone. I made sure the materials they were using were reasonably available.		
Uses a routine	4	I used the usual thing – 'Hands behind backs' – it's a gimmick I use. I brought them together as I usually do with their prayer, said 'Good morning'.	2	1
Seating	7	I made a point of pulling the desks apart. I used the system of having one pupil sitting either side of me.		
Miscellaneous	4	I never made a competition out of it. I did accept that example from that pupil. I kept my temper fairly well this afternoon.	4	2
Uses sanctions	5	I sent (him) back to the classroom area because he had been misbehaving in the Wendy House. I said, 'Oh, you're not sitting up nicely so someone else will do it'.		

absence. It is interesting to contrast the relatively small amount of teacher discourse about sanctions, warnings and verbal rebukes with the salience of these actions for pupils. In Chapter 6 we see that about 44 per cent of the actions identified by pupils as getting the class to work well concerned what we have classified broadly as control and rules. This includes actions such as verbal rebukes and using sanctions and warnings.

The third point is that non-verbal actions may be underrepresented. A look, a raised eyebrow, a shrug of the shoulders or a long pause and eyes raised heavenwards were examples of non-verbal communication which we observed but to which the teachers made little or no reference. Our research approach may have encouraged teachers to concentrate on their talk, although we have a category of the teacher using her position in the classroom to get the class to work well. Teachers talked about, for example, sitting in the middle of the room so that they could see what was going on, or deliberately standing in front of the whole class to convey authority. Again, a different research approach might have elicited different responses from the teachers.

Lastly, as in the data from pupils, the mention of rewards and praise in the teachers' discourse is very sparing, only eight of the 198 actions fell into this category. Once again we note the consistency of these data with other research findings.

We can arrange the fifteen categories into clusters of actions taken by the teachers to show the patterns to their actions more clearly. Our view of clusters is shown in Table 5.2. There are five main groups: Setting the framework; Responding to the threat of disruption; Explaining; Personal relationships; and Other. The table also shows the categories we have used to produce these clusters and the distribution of teachers' actions across them.

This gives us a general but not watertight division of the teachers' classroom actions. For example, seating was occasionally used as a reaction to problem behaviour – such as moving a pupil to sit beside the teacher – and in that sense is not, strictly speaking, setting the framework. The clustering gives us a clearer picture of the balance between general planning actions designed to avoid opportunities for disruption and actions taken in response to disruption. The emphasis on preparation and planning has already been discussed. Of equal importance, it seems to us, is that a quarter of the comment from these experienced teachers about getting the class to work well concerns dealing with disruption. This suggests that good discipline is not something which is established early on in the school year with the teacher's specific class and that is the end of it. Rather, it is something which teachers work at constantly, reinforcing their rules and routines when the situation demands it. As the research for the Elton Committee showed, most teachers have to deal with minor acts of disruption every day. The research also points out that the cumulative effect of this upon teachers' morale ought not to be underestimated.

Table 5.2: Clusters of teachers' actions to get the class to work well

Cluster	Category	N = 198	%
Setting the framework	Gives instructions/organises work	104	53
	Prepares/plans		
	Uses normal routine		
	Seating		
Responding to threat of disruption	Allows infringement of rules	49	25
	Observes/positions		
	Uses sanctions		
	Verbal rebuke		
	Gives warnings		
	Asks questions		
Explaining	Explains/helps	26	13
Personal relationships/ encouragement	Reward/encouragement/praise	15	8
	Uses humour		
	Personal contact		
Other	Miscellaneous	4	2

Percentages rounded off to nearest whole number

Conditions

As we pointed out in Chapter 4, the actions teachers take are profoundly influenced by the context in which they work. In trying to delineate this context we have used the concepts of conditions and goals. Let us now consider what teachers had to say about the conditions they were conscious of taking into account as influences on their actions.

When teachers talked about the conditions affecting their work, they did not only mean the terms and conditions of service associated with the profession. Rather, they referred to a whole range of influences which affected their decisions about the actions they took. As previously mentioned, such influences included their knowledge of particular pupils and the time of day in which an activity was taking place. Table 5.3 illustrates our categorisation of the conditions teachers talked about. Some of their comments are given under each category. As we will see, teachers made many more comments about conditions influencing their actions than about either their actions themselves or their goals.

Table 5.3 shows how dominant an influence is the teacher's knowledge about the class, particular groupings and about individual pupils, accounting for 37 per cent of teachers' statements about conditions influencing their actions. It would be fascinating to be able to compare these data from experienced teachers, all with many years service in their schools, with data from

Table 5.3: Conditions influencing actions

Category	Teacher Statements	N = 358	%	Category	Teacher Statements	N = 358	%
Knowledge of the pupils (references to groups or whole class)	They are all very eager for praise. With these children you are constantly having to go over things because they are babyish and immature.	77	22	**Part of a routine procedure**	I have activities I keep specifically for Fridays. This is the routine when they're doing (this kind of work)	17	5
General working conditions of the class	The first group were working on the page (to do) with money. The materials (pupils) need are there.	53	15	**The kind of work being undertaken**	I was aware the children were working on maths. We had been talking about the circus prior to that.	14	4
Knowledge of an individual pupil	She is particularly artistic. Paul can do better work.	52	15	**External to classroom conditions**	I do use the advice given by the (Education Authority)	7	2
Beliefs/ generalisations/ theories	I believe a look is more effective than a verbal rebuke. General instructions lead to chaos. You have to give specific instructions.	44	12	**The teacher's feelings**	There were several occasions when I felt I could have strangled them. I was fed up.	6	2
Signs of pupil misbehaviour or difficulty with work	Some of them were giggling or sniggering. One wee boy came out twice and asked for help.	40	11	**Numbers in class or group**	It's just the sheer numbers, the size of the class. You just can't do it altogether (as a whole class)	2	1

(continued)

Table 5.3 (*continued*)

Time	23	Well, it is the start of term. We (got) plenty of time to talk about the trip to the beach.	6	**Miscellaneous**	The situation was that if things had got out of hand we would have lost that part of the day. I had praised them already for looking neat and clean. 5 1
Teachers' previous experience	18	Experience tells me that it works to have everything prepared. I have had experience of classes getting out of hand in that sort of situation.	5		

beginning teachers. We speculate that beginning teachers would not make such extensive reference to their knowledge of the pupil or the class, simply because they would have been unable to build up such knowledge. It would also be interesting to discover if experienced teachers, newly appointed to a school, referred to their lack of knowledge about the pupils and class as a handicap in their decisions about the most appropriate actions to get the class to work well.

As with teacher actions, we do not know if teachers talked about the conditions which were most salient for them or simply those they found easiest to articulate. It was interesting, for example, that only two references were made to class size, given the recent prominence of this issue in the press. Three of the eight classes had twenty-six to thirty pupils and two, being composite classes, were smaller, around twenty-two to twenty-four. The remaining class sizes were thirty, thirty-one and thirty-three. It may be, of course, that the teachers accepted their class size as given and did not think it worthy of comment as they were used to coping with this.

It is also worth pointing out how infrequently external-to-classroom factors were mentioned. Again, we do not know if this was a consequence of our research approach, which focused on the classroom, or if, in thinking about their teaching, our primary teachers conceptualised it as that which happened in their classrooms.

Table 5.4:   Clusters of conditions

Condition	N = 358	%
Teacher knowledge of class; of pupils; of topic; past experience	161	45
General organisation Working condition of the class; time; numbers; external factors; signs of pupil misbehaviour; routines.	142	40
Personal Beliefs/theories; feelings.	50	14
Other	5	1

If we group conditions into clusters (Table 8.4) we can see the balance among the kinds of conditions teachers take into account, influencing their actions. Of course, any categorisation is bound to be somewhat arbitrary and we are conscious that we have grouped together rather different kinds of teacher knowledge. Indeed, one might argue that some of our components of the general organisation category represent what Eraut (1988) has called, in a different context, 'situational knowledge'. What is clear, however, is the large number of different kinds of conditions which impinge on classroom teaching. What is also clear is that learning about some of these conditions relies heavily on direct classroom experience. The kind of knowledge of pupils and classes which teachers mentioned so frequently was knowledge about the particular, the abilities, attitudes and likely reactions of a particular class or pupil, in their school. It was not abstract theoretical knowledge about infants or about child development. We are not implying that teachers did not have such knowledge or, indeed, that they did not use it. We might speculate that it provided a framework for their specific knowledge of such and such a pupil in such and such a class in such and such a school. Such a framework remained implicit and it was the particular which dominated teachers' discourse. We discuss this further at the end of the chapter.

Goals

So far we have concentrated on the influence of a wide range of conditions on teachers' actions. However, as was evident in Chapter 4, the goals which teachers have for their lessons also influence the actions they take. They may have a goal for the whole class or a group of pupils, for example, to finish a piece of work, produce an artefact such as the albatross mentioned earlier, or perform a play. A goal for an individual pupil might be to get him or her to answer a question or to take the lead in organising a group activity. Our teachers usually had more than one goal for their pupils in any given class-room activity but what was striking about these goals was that they were almost always expressed in terms of what their pupils were doing. Brown and McIntyre (1989), in their study of teachers' craft knowledge, identified a similar phenomenon:

> [Teachers'] dominant goals, and the terms in which they first evaluated the lessons, were concerned with establishing and maintaining what we call a normal desirable state of pupil activity [NDS] in the classroom. . . . The lesson was seen as satisfactory so long as pupils continued to act in those ways which were seen by the teacher as routinely desirable.
>
> (p33)

Brown and McIntyre go on to point out that what was seen as normal and desirable by one teacher could be quite different from the NDS of another. We have found this concept of normal desirable state helpful in categorising the goals which teachers talked to us about. Of course, we had already suggested to them one NDS, that of getting the class to work well. However, the teachers talked more specifically about what this meant to them. A couple of examples will give an idea of the diversity of what were seen by teachers as routinely desirable ways for pupils to behave. The first teacher conveys that her normal desirable state of pupil activity during a science lesson is that the children should work in groups and come to the correct conclusions on a topic through debate and discussion.

In this science lesson . . . an important function of this form of grouping is that they are self-disciplined . . . I listen very closely to the conversations to hear if the children are reaching the right conclusions. . . . If they reach them through discussion and experiment without me having to tell them, that's far more advantageous to them because they've discovered it for themselves. . . . It is important that they complete the experiments . . . and then go on to worksheets on each experiment.

The second teacher explains that she played some music to the pupils as she wanted them to paint. She believed they would find inspirations in the music. Her normal desirable state for pupils painting was that it should be preceded by a discussion about music and that the music should be playing while the children were painting.

Today I was playing music because I wanted the children to paint. . . . I feel it helps if they can still listen to the music while they're painting – it gives them more ideas . . . it brings back things that we've been discussing.

These two extracts give examples of the diverse nature of NDS and of the diverse actions which are taken to establish and maintain them. We were able to classify 117 of the teachers' statements about goals as NDS. This was by far the largest single category of statements about goals and can be thought of as encapsulating the different meanings of getting the class to work well. However, Brown and McIntyre also identified another goal which teachers had for their pupils: that they should make some kind of progress. Brown and McIntyre (op. cit., p. 39) make the distinction between NDS and progress in the following way: 'NDS involves something being maintained without change over a period of time; progress introduces a development aspect which contrasts with the steady state of NDS'. They go on to distinguish three kinds of progress: the development of pupils' knowledge, understanding, skills or other attributes; generating a product such as an artefact or a performance; and progress through the work. We identified these goals from our data, too, but they were very much fewer in number than the NDS. We identified only five progress goals, compared to the 117 NDS.

Brown and McIntyre do not quantify their analysis of NDS and progress goals although they say that the latter were less numerous that the former. They were, however, talking to teachers more generally about what they valued in their teaching while we were concentrating on getting the class to work well. It is, therefore, not surprising that our teachers should talk more about their NDS than about progress. One example of a progress goal is given below, where the teacher talks about model making.

Now, what else did we do? The models that they're doing . . . I told them where to go and get the materials because they're still not familiar with where everything is kept . . . Once these have been made, perhaps during this week sometime, we'll put up a display [indicating] 'This is so and so's machine [and] this is what it does'.

Brown and McIntyre indicate a two-way relationship between NDS and progress goals. That is, normal desirable states are often a pre-condition for progress. For example, a class has to know how to behave appropriately in a science lesson so that the pupils can make progress from experiment to note-taking and writing up results, thereby making progress through the work. However, sometimes progress goals are a way of establishing and maintaining an NDS. The clearest example of this comes from an infant teacher who talks about training infants so that her NDS of group work and turn-taking by pupils can be established.

> I'm trying to train them now that if I'm working with a group, then they have to get on with what they're supposed to do. And when I've finished with [a particular group], I'll be ready to see them. . . . Amanda, too, has to learn that I'm not here just for her – that there are another thirty-two that have to have some attention.

In addition to NDS and progress goals, we were able to identify three other kinds of goals from our teachers' statements: avoidance goals; reward and praise goals; and punishment and displeasure goals. These were mentioned very infrequently and may be thought of as sub-sets of NDS. We mention them here principally because we also identified them in secondary teachers' discourse and they may be of interest to other researchers.

We counted twenty-six avoidance goals. These were statements about the purposes of action taken to avoid something happening. For example: 'I separated the children so that they wouldn't get on one another's nerves, in these hot, sticky circumstances'. (It was a particularly warm, sunny day.)

Both punishment and reward goals were very few in number, only two in each category. An example of a punishment goal below describes a teacher's goal to 'squash' a new boy to her class who was impertinent. She felt that if he 'got away with' bad behaviour it would spread to others in the class and she wanted to avoid this happening. This is one example, among many, of teachers holding two or more goals simultaneously and of these influencing actions. Her action was to send the boy to the headteacher.

> Andrew had been swearing at the girls and when I told him off he just stood there. So I sent him down to [the headteacher] and he got some sort of reaction. . . . So with Andrew, I'm not going to mess about in the classroom with him. I've got to have someone outside the classroom [deal with him] because if the others see that I'm getting nowhere, they're going to think, 'Who's going to be next?'

The reward goals included statements about actions taken to reassure shy pupils or give them confidence.

The tiny number of goals in the punishment category is a little surprising given that almost a third of teachers' actions were classified as responding to the threat of disruption. This suggests two things to us. First, it reinforces our view that the kinds of disruption which teachers had to deal with were relatively minor. As already indicated, this is borne out both by our own observation data and by many other studies. The second point follows from the first: that in dealing with the minor acts of disruption, teachers only rarely wish to punish pupils. Rather, their actions are directed at getting the individual pupil or the class as a whole back to the teacher's normal desirable state of activity. Again, this is a picture which seems plausible. Our schools are not staffed by sadists whose aim is punishment for its own sake. Punishments are there to get the class to work well and it is in this sense that our data about punishment and, indeed, about reward goals should be understood. An alternative explanation, of course, is that teachers would not have revealed punishment goals to us, feeling that they would be unacceptable. All we can say is that in talking to us over the course of a fortnight's classroom observation, we are sure teachers were not camouflaging their sadistic tendencies!

We have spent some time discussing goals and our categorisation of them because we felt that this was a more difficult area than that of actions and conditions. The categorisation of actions and conditions have been presented in tables and, to complete the picture, Table 5.5 illustrates the goals which influenced teachers' actions.

Table 5.5: Goals influencing actions

Goal	N = 154	%
Normal desirable state	117	76
Avoidance	26	17
Progress	5	3
Reward/praise	2	1
Punishment/displeasure	2	1
Other	2	1

Percentages rounded to nearest whole number

Do goals and conditions predict actions?

We began our research in the belief that effective discipline was highly context specific, that what worked for one teacher in one school would not necessarily work for another teacher in a different school. The data from our eight teachers working in four different schools seemed to confirm this. However, since we had been able to classify actions, goals and conditions we looked for patterns among the three. Were particular goals and conditions associated with particular actions? The high number of normal desirable state goals made this an impossible question to answer, as normal desirable states of pupil activity meant different things to different teachers. Similarly, the kinds of conditions influencing actions were complex. The high number of conditions relating to teachers' knowledge of their classes and of their individual pupils suggested their salience for teachers' actions and goals. We know little about how teachers acquire such knowledge or, indeed, about how accurate and complete it is. Notwithstanding this difficulty in associating actions and conditions, however, the picture was further complicated since teacher actions were seldom influenced by only one condition. Typically two, three or four conditions interacted to influence a single action. In the following fairly typical extract the teacher refers to a number of conditions influencing her use of 'news time' to get the class to work well. These include her experience of the previous success of the action, her knowledge of the class (their home backgrounds and their recent trip) and her belief that getting children into a positive frame of mind helps their learning.

Researcher: What did you do during that lesson to get the class to work well?

Teacher: I think I drew them together to try and find something that was in the news this morning that they had all heard about, to try and make a common factor to tune into [leading to a piece of writing].

Researcher: Why is that important to making them work well?

Teacher: Now, why is that important? It works. I know it works. They all have a chance to talk. It kind of gets everyone into a positive frame of mind. They're all working with each other, they're interrelating, so they work. Everyone gets a chance to add a bit at a time. So, when they're set to do a particular piece of work they're not thinking 'I wanted to tell the teacher this.' . . . It's going back to the idea that . . . there are all sorts of things going on in the world. We have to get out and pay attention to other things that are happening. We're not excluding everything else just because P4 and P5 had a trip to the beach . . . [News time] gives them a chance to get something off their chests if they need to [about happenings at home] – we're very aware of [their] adverse social conditions, and [we can move beyond that to national news] . . . plus it settles them.

The complex and highly context specific nature of the interaction between teacher and pupils suggests to us that it is misguided to look for a code of practice guaranteed to make the class work well. Rather we would highlight the dominance of proactive approaches and thus the need for thorough preparation and planning, the constant monitoring required to maintain a normal desirable state of pupil activity, and the need to take into account a large number of conditions in such preparation and monitoring.

Summary

In this chapter we have tried to fill out the framework of teachers' actions, conditions and goals presented in more general terms in Chapter 4. We have stressed that teachers take a wide variety of actions to get their classes to work well and that these actions are influenced by a wide variety of conditions. Further, we have emphasised that what counts as getting the class to work well means different things to different teachers. Within all this diversity, however, certain points stand out:

- Setting the framework in classrooms to avoid the occurrence of disruption featured extensively in teachers' comments about their classroom discipline.
- Actions most commonly referred to were preparation and planning, organisation and management of the class, explaining and helping.
- One quarter of teachers' actions were devoted to dealing with disruption.
- The kinds of disruption most commonly encountered were minor but irritating, such as pupils talking out of turn and forgetting books and materials.

- Reactions to disruption involved verbal rebukes, warnings and the sparing use of more serious sanctions.
- Teachers' goals were expressed in terms of the activities of their pupils. The most common goal was a normal desirable state of pupil activity but this meant different things to different teachers.
- The conditions most commonly influencing teachers' actions were knowledge of the class and pupils.

In summarising our findings we should like to draw attention to the importance of the teachers' knowledge of their pupils as conditions influencing their actions. This seems to us to have two important implications for teaching practice. First, it suggests that student teachers need to spend time talking to experienced teachers about their classes and about the kinds of actions that are most successful with particular classes in promoting and maintaining discipline. Second, it suggests that there may be merit in student teachers spending their teaching practice in one school so that they can build up their knowledge of individual pupils and classes. It is not for us to advocate particular patterns of teaching practice. This was not the focus of the research. For example, we have no evidence to suggest that blocks of school experience juxtaposed with blocks of college experience are more or less effective than students spending part of every week in school and part in college. What our evidence does suggest is that our teachers rely to a considerable extent on their knowledge of pupils and classes as a guide to action in maintaining discipline. It seems, therefore, to be important to give students the opportunity to begin to build up this kind of knowledge so that they can consider it in the context of their more abstract knowledge about teaching and learning.

References

Brown, S. and McIntyre, D. (1989) *Making Sense of Teaching*, Scottish Council for Research in Education, Edinburgh.

Calderhead, J. (1984) *Teachers' Classroom Decision-Making*, Holt, Rinehart & Winston, London.

Clark, C. M. and Yinger, R. J. (1987) Teaching planning, in J. Calderhead (ed.) *Exploring Teachers' Thinking*, Cassell, London.

Eraut, M. (1988) Management knowledge: Its nature and development, in J. Calderhead (ed.) *Teachers' Professional Knowledge*, Falmer Press, Lewes.

Kounin, J. (1970) *Discipline and Group Management in Classrooms*, Holt, Rinehart & Winston, New York.

6
PUPILS' VIEWS ON DISCIPLINE

We have concentrated so far on what the teachers in our schools had to say about effective discipline in the school as a whole and in their classrooms. We have suggested there were important differences in emphases among the schools both in what counted as effective discipline and in the ways the schools used rules, sanctions and rewards. At classroom level, however, we have concentrated on the similarities among teachers, describing an aspect of their professional craft knowledge. Teachers' views, however, are only part of the story. Teaching is a highly interactive business and pupils' views on discipline were obviously pertinent. In this chapter we report pupils' views on classroom discipline and on school discipline.

Classroom discipline

Recent reviews of research suggest that less is written about primary school pupils' perceptions of effective teaching than about secondary school pupils' views. Much of the research on pupils' perceptions concerns ideal teachers. Pupils are typically asked to write about the characteristics of a good teacher or to rate certain characteristics. From all this work certain common ideal constructs of a good teacher have emerged. Unsurprisingly perhaps, they include explaining work clearly and being firm and fair. Our work with pupils was rather different in that we asked pupils to write about what their class teacher did to get the class to work well. Thus it focused on real teachers and their actions rather than their more general characteristics.

In each of our case-study schools, all of the P6 and P7 pupils (eleven- and twelve-year olds) were asked to write about their teachers, a total of 301 pupils, and twelve teachers in all. We had decided on the question, 'What does your teacher do to make the class work well?' because pilot work had indicated that this produced a range of responses. Our broad definition of discipline was 'creating conditions in which learning can take place' and we wanted to use a phrase which did not necessarily limit pupils to control and rule enforcement actions.

In all of the schools the pupils responded positively to the question and wrote much that was interesting and informative. We collected over five hundred statements from pupils on what their teachers did to make the class work well. While some pupils mentioned only a single action by their teachers, others mentioned three or more. Table 6.1 shows that, on average, pupils were able to generate around two comments each.

Table 6.1: Mean N of criteria per pupil per teacher

	P7	**P7**	**P6**	**P6**
Westway	1.45	1.77	1.56	
St Veronica's	1.68		1.26	
Braidburn	2.0		1.68	1.73
Oldtown	2.32	2.14	1.35	1.93

The researchers supervised the pupils' writing, following an agreed format on how to introduce the exercise and deal with questions. In addition to pupils' writing, we include, where appropriate, the views of younger pupils elicited through informal discussion.

What do teachers do to get the class to work well?

Table 6.2 lists the actions mentioned by the pupils in their five hundred statements, collated into categories. The categories are our own labels, established by a coding procedure which involved four people working from the same sample of scripts to establish coding rules. We have included examples of pupil statements under each of the categories.

The table shows that, for the most part, the pupils wrote about teacher actions and that actions ranging from rebukes and sanctions to rewarding and explaining were included. The pupil statements were made with varying degrees of specificity. For example, in the category 'enjoyment/interest', one pupil (Braidburn) comments: 'My teacher makes work interesting'. Another (Oldtown) goes into much greater detail about the ways in which the teacher makes work interesting: '[He] brings in different things to show us and lets us touch them e.g. there are snails and worms in the classroom at the moment. Last term there were crofter's clothes [he] brought in'.

Only one of the categories did not directly describe a teacher action or

Table 6.2: What does your teacher do to make the class work well?

Category Label	Example of Pupil Statement	Category Label	Example of Pupil Statement
1 Control	He always makes people know he's in charge.	8 Explains	Mrs – talks about it for a while and tells us some answers. She can make it sound easy.
2 Warns/threatens	Our teacher sometimes says we won't get football or gym if we don't behave.	9 Helps	If we are puzzled, we are told to come up and ask so we understand.
3 Work at home	If we don't work he says to take the work home.	10 Enjoyment/interest	Our teacher makes us all enjoy our work.
4 Uses sanctions	He keeps us in at playtime.	11 Personal relationships	Our class is like a big family with Mrs – like our mother.
5 Verbal rebuke	If we are noisy, the teacher tells us off.	12 Rewards/praise	She said if you work well you will get a good thing for after playtime like art or free time.
6 Tells us how to behave/work	Sometimes he tells us to be quiet because if you talk when you're working you get a lot wrong.	13 Miscellaneous	The teacher says if we don't do good, we won't get a good education.
7 Organises work	Most work is written on the blackboard. Certain places for certain things . . . (things) are all together.	14 Unclear	If I have a good breakfast.

actions; this was 'control', a general approach rather than a specification. A small percentage of pupils (1.5 per cent, see Table 6.3) saw this as important in getting the class to work well.

The 'miscellaneous' category included further purely descriptive statements which generally covered what the class did during the teaching day and also included infrequently given teacher actions. Examples of these miscellaneous statements are: 'We do writing, then we do sums from the board, then we draw . . .' and '[She] says if we don't do good, we won't get a good education'.

There were also a number of statements which were coded separately as unclear or irrelevant: 'If I have a good breakfast'. 'I think Religion makes us work well'.

An analysis of frequency of mention of actions across our 301 pupils showed that no single action dominated their perception of what their teacher did to get the class to work well. Table 6.3 gives details. There are a number of points to be made about this table. First, no single action forms more than 14 per cent of the pupils' comment, implying perhaps that pupils see teachers using a range of actions. The table shows that the most frequently occurring category is 'verbal rebukes', followed by 'tells us how to behave/work', 'explains' and 'sanctions'. In general, the table suggests a kind of carrot and stick approach with control and rule actions counterbalanced by organising and progressing through work and positive relationships.

Table 6.3:   Summary of four schools

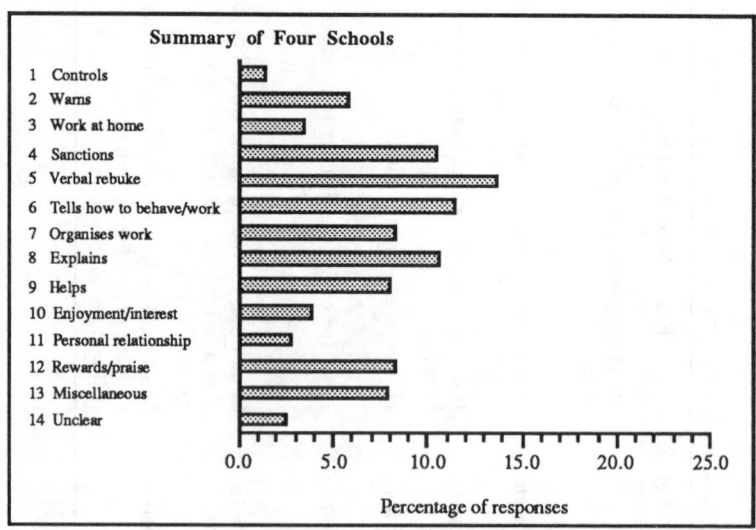

Second, the pupils clearly do not identify planning and preparation done by their teachers. In other words, they seem unaware of actions outside the classroom. However, statements about making the work interesting and enjoyable suggest that pupils may have some grasp of these aspects of the teacher's craft even though they are not labelled planning, preparation, pace and variety. Indeed, the third point to make is the absence of comment about group work, whole class teaching or individualised learning. Although 'organises work' emerged as a category, pupils' comments concerned actions related to placing materials and resources and use of the blackboard rather than specific methods.

The picture which emerges is of pupils describing teachers who set down clear instructions on how they are to work and behave and who reprimand the class when these instructions are not adhered to. Our findings mirror the picture of teachers set out by other researchers into pupils' concepts of good teaching. Previous research evidence has suggested that pupils felt that teachers had a responsibility to keep them in order. Certainly, many children seem to respond well to a controlled classroom environment. They have a positive response to a teacher who 'keeps order', is 'firm and fair', 'non-punitive' and 'not too friendly'. Our pupils seemed to conform to the notion that teachers needed to impose rules to avoid chaos and pupils expected that 'good' teachers would do just that. The following response from a P6 pupil in one of our schools illustrates this notion: 'The teacher keeps us in order by telling us what work to do and what things to do and if we did not have the teacher we would be all jumbeld (*sic*)up'.

There were few examples of teacher actions involving pupils directing their own learning or being given responsibility for organising and planning a project. We know that these activities did take place in our case-study schools and can only speculate that our method of collecting information from pupils was not conducive to eliciting these kinds of actions, perhaps because of the focus on the teacher as the originator of work implicit in the question, 'What does your teacher do to get the class to work well?'.

Are there patterns in pupil perceptions?

So far we have concentrated on the broad picture of teacher actions drawn up from the collated replies of each class. No single category of action dominated the response. We have suggested that this might indicate that teachers use a wide range of actions. However, there could be another explanation. The broad picture with its wide range of actions could be an accumulation of twelve more narrow and individually different teaching styles. For example, all of those pupils who gave the category of action 'warns' might come from the same class and be describing the same teacher. This teacher might be the only one of the twelve who was seen by pupils as using this particular action to get the class to work well. It was important, therefore, to look more closely at patterns of pupil response in the individual classrooms before accepting the broad overall picture as a valid one.

The average rate of response was 1.7 statements per pupil; 43 per cent of the pupils gave only a single comment about what their teacher did. Every classroom had its share of these singletons. Did they tend to focus on one key common feature of their teacher's approach? The short answer is 'no'. For example, in the classroom with the highest percentage of single statement responses (74 per cent), the twenty pupils so replying gave in total ten different categories of response; the highest number giving the same single category was four pupils.

What about the pupils who gave at least two comments? Did each teacher generate a pattern of matched pairs in his/her classroom, different patterns in different classrooms leading to the broad general picture? Again, this was not the case. For example, in the class which generated a particularly high number of pupil comments, there were many pairs; the highest number of pupils who repeated the same pair was six, as Table 6.4 shows.

Table 6.4: Pupil use of paired descriptions of the teacher

Oldtown – Teacher A 31 Pupils	Pairs of categories
6 pupils gave	4 + 5
3 pupils gave	8 + 9
3 pupils gave	4 + 6
3 pupils gave	3 + 6
2 pupils gave	7 + 8
2 pupils gave	5 + 6
2 pupils gave	5 + 11

Looking more closely at each class response, we found that within each class a broad range of comment was given. Pupils did not focus on one common feature if they gave just a single comment, nor did they consistently focus on the same pair of actions. Excluding the 'unclear' category of response, the twelve teachers were seen by their pupils as using anything from eight to twelve different actions to get the class to work well. The 'missing' actions from the overall list of thirteen categories were different for each teacher. We present profiles of two teachers each teaching P7 in the same school to illustrate this point.

It is clear from Table 6.5 that, as far as pupils are concerned, there is no simple recipe for getting the class to work well. Pupils perceived Teacher A as telling them how to work and behave, balancing this with explanations on how to work, giving warnings if these directions were not obeyed and sending work home if it was not completed in school. Teacher B, in contrast, is described as using verbal rebukes and sanctions to a far greater degree. Both teachers were identified by pupils as using quite a high number of 'controlling strategies' (50 per cent in each case). However, Teacher A used actions to do with 'telling pupils how to behave or work' (six) whereas Teacher B used 'verbal rebukes' (five) to a greater extent. While Teacher A was seen to use 'rewards and praise' (twelve) as an incentive, Teacher B was identified as using 'enjoyment interest' (ten).

For each of the eight teachers, then, pupils saw a range of actions; and the balance between these actions varied from teacher to teacher. Some of the

Table 6.5:   Teacher profiles at Oldtown

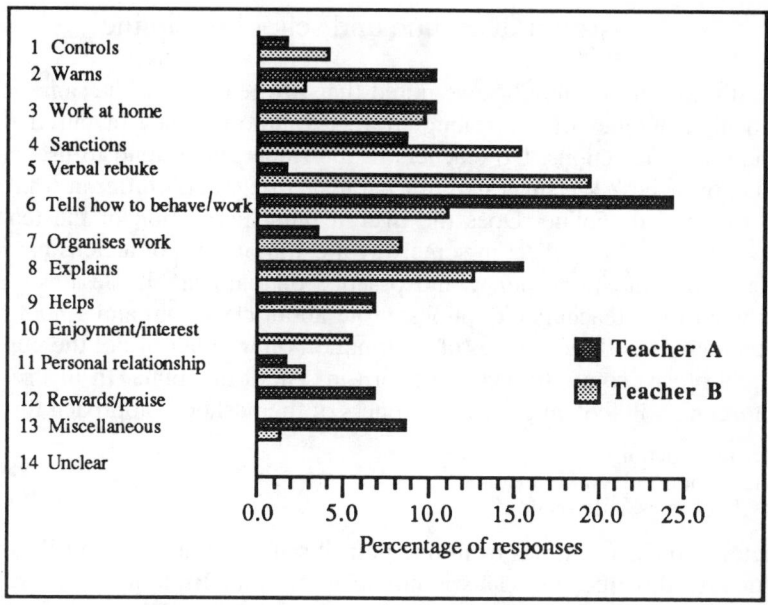

teachers seemed to have 'favourite' actions, cited by half to three-quarters of the class; but even here, the four teachers concerned also used from seven to eleven other actions. Why should this be the case? If a primary teacher is seen as behaving in a certain way by some pupils, why is this behaviour not identified in the same way by other pupils? We could speculate that the interaction between teacher and pupil meant that the teacher fitted his or her actions to the individual. In other words, the teacher catered for individual needs. However, we should also remember that the question asked of pupils was, 'What does your teacher do to make the class work well?' Of course, pupils may have been thinking about their own rather than the class response to a teacher. Overall, we can claim some commonality among pupils in identifying what teachers do. All pupils saw what we have called control and rules, organising and progressing through work and positive relationships with the teacher as components of effective discipline. However, there were differences in the balance among these components in individual classrooms. The analysis of the data to uncover patterns in pupils' responses gives a broad indication of the kinds of actions they see as conducive to getting the class to work well. These actions, together with those identified from the teachers themselves, support many of the standard texts for beginning teachers on classroom discipline by emphasising careful preparation together with active rule maintenance and a positive classroom climate. (Readers interested in investigating what other researchers have written on this topic will find useful references at the conclusion of this chapter.)

Classroom discipline and school discipline

In the discussion of Table 6.5, we noted that two teachers in the same school used a high number of controlling strategies although they favoured rather different specific actions. Do teachers in the same school tend to use similar broad approaches? We suggested in Chapter 2 that schools differ in what they count as good discipline. Does the overall pupil perception of the teachers within a given school reflect in some way a common core of actions based on the distinctive discipline policy and practice of that school? Besides writing about what their teachers did, pupils wrote about classroom and school rules. This then gives us three sources of information on whether or not the pupils in each school saw some distinctive pattern in school discipline. In this section, therefore, we will look at pupils' awareness of their school's approach through:

- teacher actions;
- classroom rules and sanctions;
- school rules and sanctions.

We intend to use examples from one pair of schools, Oldtown and Westway, to illustrate this question. This is not to imply that Braidburn and St Veronica's pupils had similar views of what counted as good discipline; all four schools had their differences and similarities, but to cover all of these would overwhelm the reader with detail. We should also add a note of caution. Pupils in P6 and P7 cannot be said to be representative of all the pupils in a school. In addition, differences in school size could have important effects. In Oldtown, for example, 119 pupils wrote about teacher actions, classroom rules and school rules; in Westway we collected data from sixty-six pupils.

Westway and Oldtown seemed to us to offer a strong contrast in their discipline policy and practice. Westway set clear standards and emphasised the need for explanation and good teacher–pupil relationships in their 'oasis in a desert of deprivation'. Oldtown also set clear standards but its traditional approach and reliance on a quiet working atmosphere was accompanied by traditional reactions to indiscipline, the rapid use of sanctions without much emphasis on their rationale.

The 'school' perception of teacher actions

Table 6.6 illustrates pupils' awareness of their school's approach by collating pupil perceptions within each school.

Westway pupils wrote relatively little about the control and rules domain of teacher actions (categories 1–6). It is striking that there was no mention of warnings and only about 5 per cent of the comment was about sanctions. Control and rules actions accounted for less than 30 per cent of pupil comment, organising and progressing through work (categories 7–10) accounted for 41 per cent and positive relationships (categories 11–12) for 18 per cent.

Table 6.6: A contrast in pupil perceptions

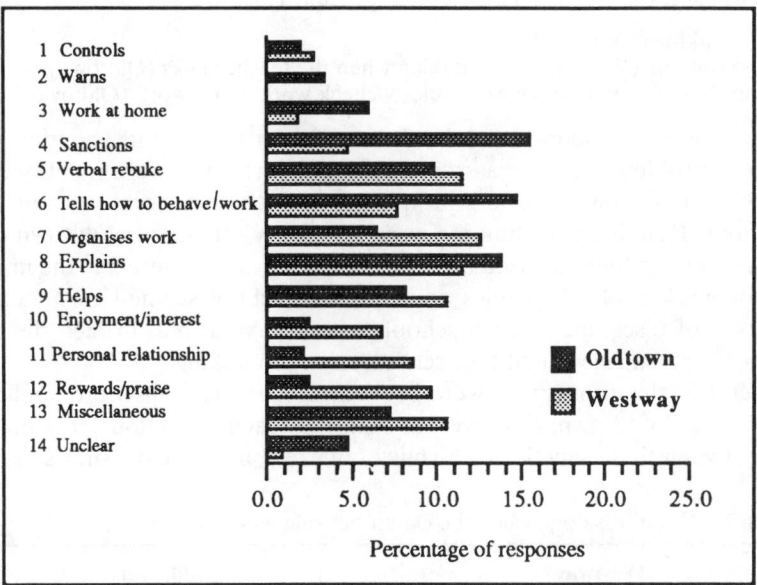

This suggests that the Westway whole school values were operationalised in P6 and P7 classrooms. Teachers got pupils to work well by emphasising, as it were, the positive aspects of control, organising work, praise and rewards and generally engendering positive pupil–teacher relationships. Where sanctions were used, it was the verbal rebuke which dominated.

The contrast with Oldtown is strong. Here control and rules actions dominated all others, engendering just over 50 per cent of the pupils' comment. Organising and progressing through work comprised 31 per cent of the comment and positive relationships less than 5 per cent. Again, it seems that the Oldtown whole school policy was operationalised in P6 and P7 classrooms. The greater reliance on sanctions in general, and punishment exercises to be carried out at home in particular, may have reflected the school's catchment area as teachers saw it, where parents could be relied upon to back up the school. We would remind the reader that about a third of the Oldtown intake was of pupils whose parents had chosen Oldtown for their children.

We would not wish to claim too much for these data, coming as they do from only P6 and P7 pupils. However, they are broadly supportive of the differences between Oldtown and Westway, reported in Chapter 2. Pupils' views on classroom rules and sanctions provided further evidence for these differences.

Classroom rules and sanctions

In both Westway and Oldtown, about 50 per cent of the pupil comment about classroom rules concerned only three rules; the other 50 per cent concerned a very wide variety of different miscellaneous 'rules' such as 'don't tip your chair' or 'don't tell tales'. The three important rules were:

- no talking (both schools);
- no running (Westway); stop talking when the teacher talks (Oldtown);
- no shouting (Westway); work rules – check work, finish work (Oldtown).

Westway was the open-plan school, therefore running and shouting were potential problems in the classroom setting. Work rules were mentioned by Westway pupils, but were less prominent than these general rules of pupil behaviour. Running and shouting were less likely offences in Oldtown classrooms; the rules there focused on a quiet working atmosphere and the importance of work itself. The rules cited in each school seemed to match the definition of discipline in each school to some extent but, in fact, the most commonly given rule (in all four schools) was 'no talking'.

When the classroom rules were broken, similar sanctions were applied in Westway and Oldtown. However, as with the teachers' actions, it is the balance between these sanctions which is of interest, as Table 6.7 shows.

Table 6.7: What was done when the classroom rule was broken?

Westway	Oldtown
Verbal rebuke (36%)	Punishment exercises (41%)
Kept in at playtime (19%)	Verbal rebuke (30%)
Punishment exercises (12%)	Kept in at playtime (5%)
Sent to headteacher (6%)	Confiscating toys (4%)
Moved to another seat (5%)	Sent letter to parents (3%)
Letter sent to parents (5%)	Sent to headteacher (1%)
Miscellaneous (9%)	Miscellaneous (4%)
No rule broken (3%)	No rule broken (6%)
Don't know/unclear (5%)	Don't know/unclear (5%)

At Westway, only 12 per cent of pupils mentioned punishment exercises as a sanction, whereas 41 per cent of the Oldtown pupils reported this. The other marked difference was in the use of detention at playtime. Of course, the differences in use of these two sanctions undoubtedly reflected factors other than how teachers in the school defined discipline. Westway teachers might realistically expect a poor return of punishment exercises, and in consequence see playtime detention as a more effective sanction. Nevertheless, Westway teachers had explained that good discipline rested on pupils' understanding the reasons for rules, and that verbal admonitions most often included explanations; presumably punishment exercises could not do so as effectively. Oldtown teachers, on the other hand, may have felt that rapid and visible sanctions such as punishment exercises fitted their traditional approach and that they could rely on most parents to ensure they were completed.

Our final piece of data on pupils' views being consonant with their schools' views of discipline concerns their perceptions of school as distinct from classroom rules and sanctions.

School rules and sanctions

It seemed to be more difficult in all our case-study schools for pupils to write about the school rules which affected them most. In each of the schools, around 10 per cent of the pupils found the question difficult to answer. We might speculate that the classroom is a more immediate environment for the pupils or that teachers focus on the rules of the particular classroom as a way of conveying general school rules. However, the pupils who did write, wrote very similarly about the school rules which affected them most. The most commonly given rule in each school was that pupils were not allowed to be in certain areas at certain times. Running in corridors, dangerous games and fighting were also prohibited in both schools, according to groups of 8–15 per cent of pupils. Many of the rules quoted were miscellaneous, covering prohibitions such as 'no litter', 'no football scarves' and 'no drinks in glass bottles'. About 7 per cent of the pupils in Westway and in Oldtown identified these rules. Very few pupils in either school, or indeed in any of the four schools, quoted a positive rule such as 'be nice to people'. Most rules were conveyed as prohibitions, as 'do nots'. As far as the pupils were concerned, school rules seemed to be a consistent reflection of school in general rather than their own school in particular. We will return to this point later.

Where we did find differences was in how the pupils reported the staff as dealing with the breaking of school rules, as Table 6.8 shows.

Table 6.8: What was done when the school rule was broken?

Westway	Oldtown
Verbal rebuke (31%)	Punishment exercises (33%)
Kept in at playtime (29%)	Verbal rebuke (13%)
Punishment exercises (10%)	Kept in at playtime (7%)
Sent to headteacher (4%)	Sent to headteacher (37%)
Parents informed (2%)	Parents informed (3%)
Miscellaneous (9%)	Miscellaneous (13%)
No rule was broken (6%)	No rule was broken (8%)
Don't know/unclear (8%)	Don't know/unclear (15%)

The overall pattern of sanctions for whole school rule breaking is similar to that for classroom rules, for both Westway and Oldtown. The headteacher in Oldtown seemed to play a more prominent role in the school rather than the classroom context. In Westway, the headteacher seemed marginally more visible to pupils in the classroom rather than school context. These differences probably reflect both the different managerial relationships, which we discussed in Chapter 3, and the architecture of the school. In terms of sanctions relating to a school definition of what counts as discipline, the same argument could be made for distinctive patterns between the schools as was made in the discussion of the classroom data. The steady reliance of Westway on 'verbal rebukes' and detention and of Oldtown on 'punishment exercises' seemed to reflect their different approaches to promoting discipline.

A pupil is a pupil

The preceding section has argued that different schools are seen as operating in different ways by their pupils. Westway and Oldtown appeared to provoke different responses when the pupils wrote about their teachers' actions and, to some extent, when they wrote about classroom and school rules. However, as we pointed out, there were also marked similarities of pupils' viewpoint across all the schools. For example, the salience of 'no talking' as a classroom rule was evident when we asked P6 and P7 pupils to write about which classroom rules affected them most. Even the youngest of pupils described the 'being quiet' rule as an important one. The following excerpt from an interview illustrates how a group of P2 pupils talked about this rule:

> Researcher: What other rules in the class do you have then?
> Michael: You're not allowed to count with your fingers . . .
> Researcher: Is that a rule?
> Gregor: Well, you are – but just a wee bit.
> Kimberley: You're allowed if you whisper, but not if you say it loud.
> Researcher: So it's all right if you do it quietly? Is that right?
> Gregor: Yes, because you might do that and talk instead . . . And, if the teacher's talking to [AHT] or [HT] you've got to whisper.
> Kimberley: And if you want to talk to the teacher, you've got to wait 'til the teacher's finished talked – not terrupt [interrupt]

In each school the largest percentage of pupils writing about rules felt that the 'no talking' rule affected them most. 'Talking in class' was also seen by the largest number of pupils in each school as the classroom rule most frequently broken. Pupils went on to explain with much seriousness that the reason this rule affected them was that it prevented them engaging in an activity which they enjoyed, namely 'chatting to my friends'. There was little element of complaint about this. The natural way of things as far as these pupils were concerned was that children enjoyed talking and it was the job of the teacher to curtail this activity so that they could get on with their work. This confirms earlier work by Cullingford (1988, p. 3) who suggested that: '. . . the children seem to stand firm in the belief that they need to have rules imposed upon them, and, thus, they learn about the realities of the world through the acceptance of inevitable rules'.

It was also interesting to note that almost all pupils across the four schools expressed the classroom rules in negative terms. The rules were expressed as 'no talking', 'no talking when teacher is talking', 'no running about'. In the same way, pupils gave prohibitive school rules such as 'not to play in the toilet at break', 'no climbing on the wall', 'no running in the corridor'. As with the classroom rules, there was a general acceptance of the need for school rules. Most of the pupils across our schools explained that the rules affected them in that sometimes they were difficult to adhere to: 'I forget and I run in the corridors, then I get in trouble'. They also suggested that the rules often restricted what they enjoyed doing. This was usually reflected in what the boys said about rules which interfered with their game of football: 'You're not allowed to go and get the ball, so we have to stop playing'. 'The rule is that you can't play on the grass in the winter – and we're not allowed the balls in the playground'.

However, pupils also suggested that they realised some rules were there for their own safety. For example: 'People would get hurt if you ran in the corridors'. 'Breaking this rule [fighting] is dangerous . . . people could get hurt'.

How did pupils see rule-breaking and its resolution?

Besides being asked about rules and sanctions, pupils were asked to write about whether rule-breaking incidents were resolved successfully. The question was, 'Did things work out well?' This question was a difficult one for pupils. For both classroom and school applications there was a marked drop-out rate and a fairly confused response, despite step-by-step instructions. We do not intend to present all the data, but to offer points which illustrate how pupils seemed to think of discipline.

In all four of our schools, pupils were more certain that things had worked out well in the classroom than they were of school misbehaviour and its resolution. Much of the response was couched in very black-and-white terms. An incident was dealt with successfully when: 'They learned their lesson'. If things did not work out well, the outcome was unsuccessful because: 'She still does it'. Pupils in St Veronica's, in particular, took a very hard line in judging a successful outcome. This school was the only one of the four where a greater percentage of pupils judged the outcome of dealing with school indiscipline as unsuccessful (42 per cent) rather than successful (31 per cent). The reasons given for this lack of success were that pupils continued to break the rules or that punishments given were not severe enough; more rarely, that the punishment was too severe or the rule itself was unfair. Perhaps pupils in St Veronica's expected perfectibility of their schoolmates?

In fact, in all four schools there were pupils who gave more sophisticated responses:

> The boy does not get better but the teacher had learned to handle it and does not get cross with the rest of us.

> Our school is the same as any other school. I think all schools have problems with certain pupils.

On the whole, the pupil response to rule-breaking was a moralistic one of retribution following on the 'crime'. This accords with the views of a number of writers in this field (Kohlberg, 1983; Nash, 1976; Cullingford, 1988). However, the pupil views on rules and rule-breaking also carried some definition of what classroom and school discipline was for and why good discipline was needed.

Means and ends – why is discipline needed?

Pupils were not asked to write directly about what discipline was for: nevertheless, many of them gave direct evidence of their views: 'If you're not talking you can get on with what you're doing'. 'If we talk and carry on we will not know the work we should know'. This view of discipline in the classroom as a means to an end, 'so the class can get on with the work', was common to pupils in all four schools. Good discipline was facilitative. In a similar way, school rules were a means to an end, to ensure the safety and well-being of pupils and to protect the fabric of the school: 'All the [school] rules are made for our safety'. 'If there was no [litter] rule, our school would be a dump and no one would come to our school'.

Very few pupils saw any element of personal benefit in keeping to the rules, other than getting on with the work. A small minority gave such comments as: 'It teaches you good habits'. 'You have to learn to keep your temper'.

As we suggested earlier, most pupils seemed to see rules as a structure whereby the teachers quite understandably attempted to curtail normal childish activities. This seemed to be acceptable as long as the rationale itself was getting on with the work; most pupils seemed to think that work was a good thing, and that they were occupied in purposeful work.

Conclusion

In this chapter we have discussed pupils' views on rules, sanctions and 'what their teachers did to get the class to work well', drawing attention to similarities and differences among the four schools.

We found a shared view of rules in that pupils generally viewed these as a form of constraint. Their portrayal of rules tended to be couched in negative terms as a list of 'do nots'. However, this constraint was also seen as a natural and acceptable responsibility of the teacher. These findings largely mirror earlier research by Morrison and McIntyre (1969) and more recently by Cullingford (1988) which has suggested that pupils felt that teachers had a responsibility to keep them in order and valued those teachers who did so.

We examined the degree to which there were differences in ways pupils described discipline operating in their own schools. It was clear that when teachers operate rules and sanctions in particular ways pupils are well aware of this. We saw how the operation of rules and sanctions at two contrasting schools was clearly evident to the P6 and P7 pupils. The idea that senior pupils in primary schools are able to reflect on the system operating within these schools will come as no surprise. The degree to which pupils' views about discipline can be collected and taken into account may be something for schools to consider.

Pupils' views on what their teachers did 'to get the class to work well' were also considered, revealing a wide range of actions which pupils saw as effective. While there was a certain amount of commonality in what pupils wrote about teachers' actions, there were also important differences. We found that pupil descriptions largely mirrored what teachers said about the discipline system. In other words, the pupil data was broadly supportive of the ways teachers described discipline as operating.

References

Cullingford, C. (1988) School rules and children's attitudes to discipline, *Educational Research*, 30, 1, pp. 3–8.

Davies, B. (1979) Children's perceptions of social interaction in school, *Collected Original Resources in Education*, 3, 1.

Docking, J. W. (1987) *Control and Discipline in Schools: Perspectives and Approaches Second Edition*, Paul Chapman, London.

Johnstone, M and Munn, P. (1987) *Discipline in School: A Review of 'Causes' and 'Cures'*, Scottish Council for Research in Education, Edinburgh.

Kohlberg, L. (1983) *Essays on Moral Development: Vol II The Psychology of Moral Development*, Harper & Row, San Francisco.

Kyriacou, C. (1986) *Effective Teaching in Schools*, Basil Blackwell, Oxford.

Marsh, P. Rosser, E. and Harre, R. (1978) *The Rules of Disorder*, Routledge & Kegan Paul, London.

Morrison, A. and McIntyre, D. (1969) *Teachers and Teaching*, Penguin, London.

Musgrove, F. and Taylor, P. A. (1965) *Society and the Teacher's Role*, Routledge & Kegan Paul, London.

Nash, R. (1976) Pupil expectations of their teachers in M. Stubbs and S. Delamont (eds.) *Explorations in Classroom Observation*, Wiley, Chichester.

Wragg, E. C. (1981) *Class Management and Control*, Macmillan, London.

Wragg, E. C. (ed.) (1984) *Classroom Teaching Skills*, Croom Helm, Beckenham.

7
PARENTS AND EFFECTIVE DISCIPLINE

It has long been recognised that parental involvement is an influential aspect of school effectiveness. The importance of parents in their children's academic success was summed up by Hargreaves *et al.* (1975) as follows:

> For very many years we have known, both from well established research findings as well as from common sense, that parental commitment is a cornerstone of the school's success. If parents are interested in their children's schooling, if they are supportive of the school's endeavours, if they act in partnership with teachers, then the children will achieve more in school.

(p.14)

Indeed, parental involvement is seen as so beneficial that various practical approaches for schools to increase such involvement have been persuasively put forward. These approaches range from ways of improving direct communication between home and school about pupils' progress and more general school matters, to signed understandings between parents and schools about their respective duties and obligations in children's schooling. Research has suggested that parental involvement has positive effects not only on children's learning but on their behaviour. A letter home to parents, a parent being asked to come to the school, or a child being placed on 'report' with a parent having to sign a behaviour card, are examples of actions heartily disliked by pupils. While the rhetoric about the need to improve home–school relations has often invoked the notion of partnership, the reality has more typically been that parents are called upon to support the school's way of doing things. Whether this will change, and we will see a much more direct influence of parents on school life as a consequence of recent legislation, is open to conjecture. There is no doubt that this is the intended consequence of such measures as the Education No. 2 Act of 1986, and the Education Reform Act of 1988 in England and Wales. Scotland has seen similar legislation in the shape of the School Boards (Scotland) Act (1988) and the Self-Governing Schools etc. Act (1989). These Acts enhance (or, in Scotland, establish) specific rights for school governors, devolve the financial management of schools to governing bodies and extend the rights of parents to choose the schools their children will attend.

At the time of the research, the impact of these legislative changes had yet to be felt. The general picture of parental involvement was that it was left to the initiative of individuals, in our schools predominantly the headteacher. What kind of parental involvement in discipline did our schools try to promote? At policy level, the schools were very similar, exhorting parents to support them in their endeavours to educate their children. In practice, however, there were important differences among the schools in the ways they promoted parental involvement in discipline. It seemed to us that these differences were directly connected to the expectations the schools had of their pupils, discussed in Chapter 2. This has led us to formulate the key idea that: the school's expectations of its pupils affect the extent and quality of its involvement with the pupils' parents.

Most of this chapter is concerned with the different ways in which schools might involve parents in promoting discipline and the consequences of this. However, it is as well to remember that our case-study schools had several important features in common as far as involving parents was concerned. We suspect that these features are common to the vast majority of schools. We discuss these features first and speculate about their consequences for discipline policy and practice before looking at different kinds of approaches to involving parents.

Who decides what counts as good discipline: teachers or parents?

The most obvious similarity among the schools was that they set the standards of pupil behaviour and parents were expected to ensure that their children conformed to those standards. The school brochures, for example, all urged parents to comply with the school's discipline policy and to support the school if there was a problem with their child.

> Certain standards of behaviour are required for the benefit of all the children and it is hoped you will continue to support the school in the maintenance of these standards.
>
> (Westway brochure)

> Discipline is necessary to make our school function smoothly, efficiently and, most important of all, happily. Certain qualities are needed to ensure this happens. These are tolerance, politeness, good manners and respect for others and for their property. . . . We ask your cooperation and support in developing these qualities and sustaining our code of discipline and behaviour.
>
> (Braidburn brochure)

The other schools' brochures similarly enjoined the parents to support the discipline of the school and indicated the measures or sanctions which would be used if standards were not met:

> Parents should be aware that persistent breaches of discipline by a child can lead to the pupil concerned being suspended from school for a period of time.
>
> (St Veronica's brochure)

> Serious and continuous cases of indiscipline will necessitate the Headteacher meeting with parents so that an appropriate course of action can be agreed. . . . We would stress that it is vital that both home and school co-operate to achieve the above [standards of discipline].
>
> (Oldtown brochure)

As far as we are aware, none of the schools had made any attempts to involve parents in discussions about school discipline policy. Parents had made no contribution to establishing school rules, for example, or the sanctions to be applied when rules were broken. If parents were seen as partners in discipline, then they were very junior partners, expected unquestioningly to support the school.

The notion of parents as junior partners was most strikingly apparent in relations between infant teachers and parents of children in the earliest stages of primary. Contact was typically informal, relaxed and fairly extensive. Most of the infant teachers in our case-study schools knew at least one member of the family, usually the mother, of all the pupils in their classes. These teachers explained how easy it was to have a brief word with parents as they came to collect or deliver children. Many of the overheard discussions between infant teachers and parents concerned social training where the implication was that the parent would reinforce the school's values. For example, an infant teacher might say to the mother of a five-year-old collecting her child at the end of the school day, 'He didn't want to share his coloured pencils today'. The mother might reply, 'Didn't he? Oh dear! Peter, why wouldn't you share your pencils with William? You know you mustn't be selfish'. Here, teacher and parent are united in reinforcing the idea that sharing things is a good way to behave. Keeping belongings to yourself is a bad way to behave. Infant teachers frequently remarked that parents had significant and useful knowledge about their children which they were eager to pass on. Such knowledge included the child's likes and dislikes, home circumstances and special events such as birthdays or outings. Yet these informal contacts between teacher and parent gradually disappeared as the child progressed through the primary. Are there ways in which schools can build on the contacts they establish with parents of infants, in the later stages of primary schools? More fundamentally, are there ways of involving parents directly in establishing the school's values?

The primacy of the school in setting standards to which parents were expected to conform was also reflected in the fact that contact between school and parents was school-led. Almost without exception, teachers in our case-study schools took the lead in contacting parents, whether in the context of an invitation to attend a parents' evening, to discuss their child's progress or to discuss a problem concerning their child. In all the schools the parents were asked to make an appointment to see the teachers and the first reference point was the headteacher. The only initiatives taken by parents were in fund-raising. Staff were highly appreciative of the parents' efforts, which they saw as making a significant contribution to the life and work of the school.

It is noteworthy that the one area where parents took initiatives, fund-raising, was one which did not challenge the professional autonomy of teach-ers. Parents were not involved directly in the school curriculum and there was no structured involvement of parents in, for example, topic work or projects. If parents wanted to help their children, the school was pleased, but it did not provide advice or guidance on how they might do so or on the benefits which might accrue. Nor were there any schemes such as paired reading in oper-ation, to help children with learning difficulties. Given the well-known asso-ciation between learning difficulties and disruptive behaviour, it is striking that systematic and structured attempts actively to involve parents in their children's school learning were so sparse.

In sum, therefore, the features which the schools had in common in terms of home–school contact were:

- the school defined the discipline standards to which parents were expected to conform;
- parents were expected to establish a foundation of acceptable behaviour in their children on which the school could build;
- parents were expected to act as a back-up or support to the school when a discipline problem arose;
- contact with parents was school-led;
- fund-raising activities by parents were warmly welcomed;
- parents were encouraged to help with extra-curricular activities;
- contacts with parents of infants were informal, routine and spontaneous; they grew progressively more distant as the child grew older;
- parents were not actively encouraged to contribute to their children's school learning;
- the main way of discussing pupil progress was via parents' evenings.

It seemed to us that each of our four schools was at a similar stage of growth in terms of developing parental involvement. They had begun to acknowledge the value of home–school contact but were unsure as to how to develop it and unclear about the implications of such developments. The schools were aware that legislative changes signalled fundamental changes in their typical rela-tionships with parents and they knew they would have to work at parental involvement over the coming years to extend it into new areas of school life. They were also aware that both staff and parental attitudes to involvement would not change overnight and would need continuous work. They did not underestimate the difficulty of the task.

Before moving on to the more specific ways in which the schools involved their parents in discipline matters, it is worth pausing to consider why schools have taken so few steps to involve parents actively in discipline policy. What inhibits schools from engaging in this kind of dialogue with parents? Is it a concern that it would be impossible to obtain a consensus about school rules? Yet rules of tolerance, courtesy, respect for others and so on, are fairly uncontentious and likely to be accepted by most parents asked for their opinion. It should not be too difficult for teachers to explain the rationale for proposed rules and sanctions. If it is, then perhaps the policy needs an overhaul. Is dialogue inhibited because there are no mechanisms or procedures for engaging in such dialogue? School governing bodies, school boards and parent–teacher associations are all possible ways of reaching parents, as are informal contacts. Indeed, as we shall see below, some of our schools were experimenting with ways of encouraging parents to feel welcome and not threatened by the school. Is it that schools could not make contact with the parents it really wants to involve in such dialogue – parents of problem children? Determined schools will promote such contact through home visits, although time and resources have clearly to be made available to make these a feasible proposition and a regular feature of school–home life. Is it that discipline is seen as a professional concern of teachers and that the legitimate role of parents is to back the school? We would suggest that parents are more likely to back the school if they feel they have been consulted about school discipline policy and played a part in formulating it. Many studies have shown the importance of a sense of ownership in the success of any new policy and this holds as true for parents as for teachers being asked to implement changes in curriculum and assessment policy. There is still a great trust by parents in the professional expertise of teachers. If teachers could build on this and begin to see parents as part of the solution rather than part of the problem, home–school relations could take a giant leap forward. So, a fundamental question for schools is: how far do they involve parents in formulating and reviewing discipline policy? Could they do more to promote parental involvement?

So far we have argued that there were important similarities among our schools in the assumptions they made about parental involvement in discipline, namely to sustain the school's view, and that this assumption was part of a larger view of home–school relations where teachers as the professionals made the decisions, and it was for the parents not to interfere but to support the school in its endeavours. These broad similarities, however, camouflaged quite marked differences in the nature and extent of parental involvement in discipline. It is to these differences that we now turn.

Are parents really welcome? Different approaches to parental involvement in discipline

Our four schools were alike in establishing discipline standards and in taking the lead in making contact with parents. They differed in tone, however, and these differences were based on school views on how interested and competent parents were to fulfil their assigned role in maintaining school discipline. Unsurprisingly, the school view of parents was strongly influenced by their beliefs about the pupils. As we discussed in Chapter 2, the social composition of the pupil intake played an important part in the kinds of rules schools emphasised, the sanctions used and the ways in which standards of behaviour were conveyed to pupils. Expectations about parents were the other side of the coin. Broadly speaking, approaches to parents ranged from trying to keep them at arm's length to welcoming and actively encouraging involvement. As might be expected, the school which was most positive about parental involvement, Braidburn, was the school where it was assumed that parents and teachers shared the same standards. The school with a history of very limited parental involvement was Westway, where large gaps between teacher and parent standards were assumed. We consider each of the schools in more detail below. However, it is important to make clear that each had a consistent and rational (in its own terms) view of the nature and extent of parental involvement which it wished to encourage. We hope by conveying something of each school's view, and the summing up of the benefits and costs in Table 7.1 at the end of the chapter, teachers will be encouraged to reflect on the situation in their own schools and to consider whether and how to involve parents in school discipline.

Braidburn

Teachers at Braidburn felt that the parents provided the pupils with a type of discipline which complemented and reinforced the discipline of school. Good behaviour was taken for granted and rules were only made explicit when a pupil or pupils had transgressed. This acceptance by staff that school and home standards were similar appeared to have a positive effect on the teacher–parent relationship. Teachers felt that they had a good rapport with parents and could rely on them for support. As one teacher commented: 'Most of them [pupils], I would think are from home backgrounds where you'd expect discipline at home . . . Any rules we have are general behaviour rules that any parent would have at home'.

The school had a thriving parents' association. Parents were involved in helping escort pupils on school trips and in many extra-curricular activities both with and without the involvement of teachers. They were used to helping out, and familar with the school and its staff. For most of Braidburn's parents, therefore, coming to the school was fairly natural. Contact was regular, informal and, of course, did not challenge teachers' professional autonomy because the parents shared the values promoted by the school. The catchment area of the school was a small town with a close-knit and stable population where a number of staff themselves lived. Teachers saw themselves as part of the wider community of the town, where 'everybody knew everybody'. Thus, when a new pupil arrived at the school, there was immediate staff-room discussion about who he was related to in the town and why his parents had moved there and so on. This appeared to indicate a desire to place the new pupil in the Braidburn context. The security that staff seemed to derive from knowing this context was one of the reasons given for what teachers saw as a homely, family type of discipline in the school. The 'family' seemed to extend to parents as well as to the pupils. A typical Braidburn view was given by one teacher: 'This is a close community. I live here. I'm known in the community . . . I've never had anything but support [from parents]'. The same teacher explained, however, that one of the costs of this closeness could be that parents might encroach and 'take advantage of the fact that this is a local school and . . . immediately pop in and complain'. She went on to say, however, that she had never had any experience of that.

Indeed, all our data from teachers in Braidburn suggested that parents backed the school if there was a discipline problem, rather than challenging the school's way of doing things. The headteacher gave the following example of prompt parental support:

> . . . He [pupil] was extremely impertinent in the dinner hall and I sent a letter home . . . The parents were straight on the phone – they [parents] really backed the staff and were really angry that this had happened . . . [they were] backing our discipline and doing the same at home.

There were also more subtle indications that teachers were looking at parents from a shared perspective. In the extract below, the implication is that teachers are parents, too, and can empathise with the slings and arrows of bringing up children; as one teacher noted:

> I think we've got a fairly good rapport with the parents at the school and I think they'd certainly show concern when they come in to talk about their child. Again, maybe there's a situation which they find difficult at home as well . . . I know myself – having youngsters – how they can behave at home and at school . . .

When staff felt that parents should be informed of an offence committed by their children, they were keen to discuss the possible reasons for pupil misbehaviour with parents. The shared assumptions about acceptable standards of behaviour made this feasible. Parents and teachers were trying to instil the same message and so, if there was a hiccup, it was sensible to engage parents in dialogue about the reasons for bad behaviour and ways of dealing with it. We were unable to talk to parents and so cannot say whether any felt remote from the school and hesitant about discussing their children's behaviour with staff. It would be surprising if all parents felt equally involved. However, staff interviews, the routine presence of parents in the school, the thriving parents' association and the active participation of parents in extra-curricular activities and school trips, all lead us to suggest that Braidburn welcomed parents and did not feel threatened by them. We suggest that this was due to shared values and, of course, a conscious effort on the school's part to encourage parent participation in school activities. Parents did not challenge the teachers' professional autonomy – the parents' association was active in fund-raising – and generally supported the school. The challenge for Braidburn was to use this firm foundation of parental involvement to extend and develop it into a more equitable partnership.

Westway

At Westway, relationships with parents were rather more distant than at Braidburn. Westway's catchment area was one of multiple deprivation, which included high levels of unemployment, single-parent families and a high incidence of petty crime. Teachers were sympathetic towards their pupils and tried to create a secure and positive environment in which pupils would be able to work, learn and enjoy the process. This was the school which was seen as an 'oasis in a desert of deprivation'. School was seen by staff as a safe haven for pupils from the vagaries of the world outside. The pupils' home backgrounds were viewed as largely deficit and parents were seen by teachers as generally well-meaning but exercising little control over their children. Therefore, it was for the school to set standards and to convey these to pupils and parents alike. Staff were far from confident about appropriate discipline standards being set at home. One example was the tendency of infants to wander away from the school playground because, in the teachers' opinion, they were unaccustomed to supervised play:

> We have to do a lot of supervision in the playground at first – because they [P1 pupils] are liable to wander off . . . The children in this area – they cross the road, just wander off, no adult with them. They're used to that, just wandering – and no one says anything to them – so we've got to teach them that they've got to stay in the playground at interval times.

This 'unsupervised wandering' by infants was observed during the research. Four- and five-year-olds were seen after school playing on waste ground with groups of pre-school children. This small example illustrates why the Westway teachers believed that an alternative code of behaviour needed to be established by the school. They hoped that the code would help educate the parents as well as the children. Thus, all parents received a copy of the school rules and were informed about procedures to be adopted if their child was absent or late. Teachers were prompt in contacting parents in such circumstances. The situation at Westway, then, was one of holding parents at arm's length, of not trusting parents to be able or willing to inculcate the standards of behaviour which the school would like to see or of backing the school if there was a discipline problem. Contact with parents tended to be limited to crises in pupil behaviour and some parents were seen as downright uncooperative or even aggressive. One member of staff summed up the situation as follows:

> Parents are not often involved. When they are asked to come to the school to discuss their child's behaviour, they, the parents, can often, initially, be quite aggressive. Then it's down to the headteacher to defuse the situation. Our headteacher is actually quite successful in this respect . . . . I would say that they [parents] are supportive of the rules within certain limits – I wouldn't say we have total back-up. . . .

Parental contact was not seen by either staff or pupils as much of a sanction in the event of wrong-doing. School was school and outside school different values operated. Since there were assumptions that teacher and parent standards were far apart and there was, correspondingly, a low level of parent involvement in the life of the school, the sanctions used were mostly within-school sanctions. A substantial cost to the school, and one recognised by the headteacher, was that pupils were inclined to develop two different codes of conduct, one for school and one for outside school. The school's aim of social training, of seeing discipline as an end in itself, was bound to fail in such circumstances. The following extract from a discussion with some Westway pupils makes this point.

Researcher: Is there trouble at those times [playtimes/lunch break]?
Fiona: No, it's at home time [3.30 pm] some people fight.
David: It's usually on Friday night, then they won't get in trouble on Saturday morning.
Researcher: Why?
David: Well, because you won't be in school on Saturday, so they fight on Friday night.
Fiona: You won't get in trouble on Saturday morning 'cos you're not there.
Researcher: So, the school is also involved with things that happen outside the school as well as what children are doing in school?
David: Yeh, you even get in trouble if you're fighting when the school isn't in, you get in trouble even then, and that shouldn't be allowed 'cos that's at night and nothing to do with the school.
Fiona: Yeh, you're not near the school.
Researcher: I see, but could it be that it's because the school is bothered about you? Even when you're out of school? What do you think?
Fiona: When you're not in school you should get to do what you want.
Researcher: Even though it's something bad?
David: Yeh, because teachers shouldn't take anything to do with say weekends or Friday nights about eight o'clock, they shouldn't have anything to do with it like if we steal from a shop, they can't do anything about it.
Paul: But they can try and stop you from doing it again.
Fiona: Say if you hit someone on Saturday night and they, the person that you hit, goes and tells the teacher and you get in trouble, that's not fair.

In our view, this graphically illustrates the consequences of not involving parents in developing and maintaining school discipline policy. However, it is easy to be critical, much harder to be constructive. What can be done in such circumstances where there seems to be a wide gulf between home and school? What Westway tried to do was to find ways of involving parents in the life of the school. The headteacher recalled how, in his first months in school, 'Any time I interviewed a parent, it was an irate parent. These were the only parents I saw in here for the first few weeks. Now, even the irate parents come in and discuss things'. He believed this change had come about through considerable perseverance and encouragement. A parent–teacher association had been recently established. He had set up specific projects to involve parents in school work, such as cataloguing library books and helping with school activities. He had made efforts to get out into the local community and persuade parents that teachers were human and approachable. In his view the library project was a good beginning to more sustained involvement: 'We had quite a good liaison with parents at the start of the year. They came in and they covered books and they sorted the library area. One parent actually took the computer and put all my 'Singing Together' songs on it and put them under headings for Environmental Studies.

The headteacher had also made a determined effort to change staff attitudes towards parental involvement. Some staff had been sceptical of parents' desire to become more closely involved with the school and had been pleased at the response to the library project. The head felt that there was still some way to go with both parents and staff. He wanted to encourage staff to listen to what parents had to say, although staff did not believe that most parents shared the same values of the school. Nevertheless, the head felt that the library project was a success:

> Parents felt up till then that they couldn't come and discuss anything with the headteacher and they came along very sheepishly. They were astonished that we would actually listen to them: they didn't realise that it was so easy to speak to folk at school – and it made a big difference to the attitudes of parents towards teachers . . .

It was a pity that the initiative had to be stopped when complaints were received from a local branch of a union about parents becoming involved in activities which would normally have been carried out by their members. The head was considering other ways of involving parents and it was clear that some of his staff were already convinced of the value of better home–school liaison.

> Many of the parents in this area have a fear of authority – police, teachers, social workers or anyone who is seen as having power over them or their children. They often come into school in an aggressive manner on the premise that attack is the best form of defence . . . I feel that if we encouraged them to participate in their child's education, to see and find out what's going on in school, they would be more relaxed and co-operative and their attitude would influence their children.
>
> (Teacher)

Westway, then, was a school with a history of minimal parental involvement. The management's task was to change both parental attitudes towards the school and teachers' attitudes towards the prospect of greater involvement by parents.

It is interesting that the head had decided on specific projects to encourage parental involvement. Several studies have shown that, given specific tasks and sufficient encouragement to develop confidence, a majority of parents are keen to help their children's education. It is also interesting that the headteacher had not taken for granted that parents would be uninterested in school life. Research has shown that notions of parental apathy need to be carefully examined by teachers; for example, it has been shown that some parents are hesitant and unsure of themselves when confronted with the structures and conventions of a school, an institution which they may well associate with failure. Westway clearly had made a start in involving parents in school life. There is no magic way of involving parents in supporting schools. Secondary schools which have been 'turned round' from having a poor reputation for discipline to having a good one, have taken sustained efforts over many years to accomplish their task and have involved parents. In our companion volume on secondary schools we draw attention to one which, in the headteacher's opinion, had taken ten years of hard work fully to effect change.

St Veronica's

St Veronica's had recently seen the appointment of a new headteacher and this appeared to be a catalyst for change in home–school relations. Relations with parents had been typically formal and distant, not because, as in Westway, different values operated, but as an aftermath of the teachers' industrial action in the early 1980s. Prior to the dispute there had been a parent–teacher association which was concerned mainly with fund-raising and helping with extra-curricular activities. Since the dispute, the level of involvement had been reduced to minimal contact evenings with parents to discuss pupils' progress. Parents, however, were generally felt to be supportive of the school standards. The school view was that parental involvement could be summed up as distant respect for and acquiescence in the school's standards of discipline. This was a state of affairs that was generally agreeable to the staff as the following excerpts from interviews with two different teachers in St Veronica's illustrate.

> Researcher: What contact do you have with parents?
> Teacher: We see parents twice a year for interview as regards the progress of their children. We occasionally see parents when they call into the school to collect their children [for appointments] . . . The only other time when we might see a parent is through notifying them if there are problems. The ordinary child in the ordinary classroom, I would see the parents twice a year – that would be my only contact.
> Researcher: And do you see this as sufficient?
> Teacher: Yes . . . I would say, if I see [most] parents twice a year that is sufficient. There is no need to see the parents otherwise.
> (First teacher)

> I think that, in general, there is a feeling that the teacher is on a slightly higher echelon but there is this respect that you had from long ago. It might be diminishing a bit now but, in general, in this school, in this community, there is this feeling 'Oh, there is a teacher'. They [parents] sort of step back a little . . .
> (Second teacher)

This respect for the authority of the school was also evident in the use of sanctions. Parents were expected to ensure that their children accepted the validity of being punished when they misbehaved. Indeed, parents were told by teachers what to do, just as the pupils were. Thus, as the following teacher makes clear, trivial complaints from parents about their children being punished would be summarily dealt with. The school was in the driving seat and parents had to accept the school's way of doing things.

> While they [senior staff] have treated parents with a great deal of respect, they also wouldn't put up with any nonsense from them. If parents came in with trivial complaints, they would be told, 'This is the standard of the school and this is how we deal with it'.

The newly appointed headteacher recognised the strength of discipline in the school. He saw the potential for moving St Veronica's, which already had a supportive though distanced relationship with parents, forward to the point of increasing parental involvement.

> Quite frankly, as a head [teacher] coming into a very well established school, you do feel the pressure to maintain these standards – there's a high expectancy from staff that these standards won't drop . . . but, in terms of parents, I think the children gain a lot of confidence in the school from having parents about. I think parents gain a lot from an open-door policy. . .

The headteacher believed that changes in home–school relations had to be carefully planned and that it was imperative to take the teaching staff along with him. He felt that there were opportunities to capitalise on the school's religious character and involve parents more actively in religious education. Some staff, too, felt that the time was right to develop home–school relations and that government initiatives in this area might help to encourage the school to move forward.

> I feel that there hasn't been much parental involvement in the past, the feeling was to keep the parents at bay . . . you know – 'There will always be trouble when the parents are involved' . . . but I don't think it's going to be like that with the new headteacher because he's already inviting parents in to organise things. I think we're going to have change and I think that will be change for the better.
>
> (Teacher)

It was interesting that St Veronica's was the only one of our primary schools to have established a school board or governing body under the School Boards (Scotland) Act (1988), at the time of the research.

Oldtown

Parental involvement in Oldtown is the most difficult of all our schools to describe. Oldtown's catchment area and the high number of parents choosing to have their children educated there, represented a parental body of stark contrasts. There was a fair mixture of parents from wealthy, upper-middle-class, professional backgrounds and parents who were poor, single parents with pressing financial and social problems. The headteacher described the pupils as follows:

> We have some children who have everything, almost too much; professional parents, large houses, every material advantage, and we have the other extreme, children

who have very little, children who have social workers, whose parent – it's one parent, usually – has been on drugs or in a mental hospital.

The school had a parents' association, which organised fund-raising and general social activities. However, in the opinion of staff, less well-off and working-class parents felt excluded from this. The school had been deeply involved in the teachers' industrial dispute in the early 1980s and most teacher–parent contact was confined to parents' evenings. The school emphasised high academic standards and in order to achieve this promoted as 'good discipline' a quiet working atmosphere. Parents were expected to agree with this and, indeed, it seemed an uncontroversial objective, even with a diversity of parents. Outside the regular parents' evenings, parents were free to contact the school about any matter of concern to them. The school's response to such contact tended to vary according to its perception of the parent involved. Thus, disadvantaged parents, who, in essence, posed little or no threat to the school's way of doing things, were treated sympathetically when they visited the school. The relationship was almost a counselling one, lending an ear, showing understanding, and trying to take home background into account if a pupil from a disadvantaged home was misbehaving. The headteacher particularly was the recipient of parents' problems, and she remarked that:

> You've got to try and be as supportive as possible to the parents as well, just to lend an ear. Sometimes they'll ask for an appointment to talk about their child, but it's really just to have an ear – but that can help the child as well. There's a great width from articulate, middle-class parents down to souls who are needing every possible help they can get.

With the more articulate parents, who had strong opinions not always supportive of the school system, a different strategy had to be adopted; in the headteacher's view:

> Here, I think, you've got to try and enforce your position on some of them. They don't like some of the things you're trying to do. They don't think their child should get a telling off – and I don't mean just from poor homes – I mean from good homes. You've got to point out to them that their child needs a row as much as anybody else's.

It seemed, therefore, that various factors contributed to a relationship with parents which was both uneasy and complex. The teachers' industrial action, the mixed clientele and the large size of the school all combined to produce slightly different applications of rules and, perhaps, a feeling of a social class division in the school. The poorer parents could feel less involved in school affairs because the parents' association was not 'for the likes of them' and could be reluctant to challenge the school's way of doing things. The more articulate upper-middle-class parents, often from academic backgrounds themselves, could be viewed as threatening school ways and challenging teachers' judgements about the application of rules and sanctions. Different parental expectations seemed to have an impact on how good discipline was defined at Oldtown and teachers were trying to deal with this by creating an overall framework of what the school brochure defines as 'fairly traditional standards of pupil work'.

Conclusion

What this chapter has tried to show is that how a school views its pupils also affects the way it deals with parents. In particular, we have tried to stress that a school's view of its pupils' home backgrounds affected its expectations of and involvement with parents. Where teachers felt confident that parents shared the school's values and supported the school in its endeavours, parental involvement was seen as non-threatening, helpful and generally a good thing, as in Braidburn. Where parents were assumed not to share the school's values and to be unreliable in backing up the school if children misbehaved, then parental involvement was distant, as in Westway.

Of course, assumptions about pupils' home backgrounds were not the only influence on teacher expectations about the extent and nature of parental involvement. Notions of teacher professionalism influenced the areas which teachers saw as legitimate for parents to take an interest. In all cases, but perhaps most starkly in St Veronica's and Oldtown, it was expected that the school would make decisions about rules, punishments and rewards. Parental involvement in challenging any such decisions was characterised as interference.

The evidence from our four schools is that fundamental assumptions were made about the nature and extent of parental involvement. In summary, these were that:

- the parents' role was to make the pupil conform to school standards by providing a grounding in decent behaviour and backing up the school if there was a problem;
- parents were useful in extra-curricular activities and in fund-raising – these were tangible signs of interest in and commitment to the school.

Where our schools differed was in the expectations they held about the efficiency of the parents' role in setting standards and their readiness to back up the school. This coloured the relationship between teacher and parent which could range from the friendly, outgoing and supportive as in Braidburn to the more cautious, distant and sceptical of Westway.

While a thorough-going review of home–school relations is beyond the scope of this study, it is noteworthy that parental involvement in schooling was not seen as including a voice in the curriculum and in how it might be taught. As earlier studies have shown, the curriculum and school and classroom organisation can have important effects for good or ill on school and classroom discipline. Whether new roles for parents as customers and school managers will be conducive to collaboration as partners in their children's school learning and in their social training remains to be seen. What is certain

Table 7.1: Benefits and costs: Different approaches to parental involvement

Westway	St Veronica's	Braidburn	Oldtown
Parents were seen as deficient in the discipline demanded by the school.	Parents were seen as acquiescent, but distanced from the discipline demanded by the school.	Parents were seen as having the same basic discipline demands as the school.	Parents were seen as being of quite different types, with different discipline standards.

HOW DID THIS AFFECT THE APPLICATION OF THE RULES?

Westway	St Veronica's	Braidburn	Oldtown
Rules were to make explicit to parents the standards of behaviour expected from their children. Rules were seen as compensating for behaviour standards not set at home. Rules had to be applied quickly, firmly and consistently to establish a secure and reliable system. Rules were not negotiated with parents.	Rules were to make explicit to parents the standards of behaviour expected from their children. Rules articulated the framework of a Catholic education, especially for the minority of pupils whose parents were seen as less aware of school standards. Rules had to be applied firmly and consistently, to reaffirm the standards of the school. Rules were not negotiated with parents.	General rules for behaviour were shared with the parents, and could be taken for granted. Specific rules were set out to meet specific school circumstances. Rules had to be applied flexibly for the good of the school community. Rules were not negotiated with parents.	Rules were to make explicit to parents the standards of behaviour expected from their children. Rules were not negotiated. Rules were framed to encourage good working behaviour, an uncontroversial school objective even with a diversity of parents. Rules had to be applied flexibly but yet had to encourage school work. Rules were not negotiated with parents.

(continued)

Table 7.1 (*continued*)

Benefits	***Benefits***	***Benefits***
• Parents were given a clear idea of the standard of behaviour expected by the school.	• Parents understood that the school's values reflected the Catholic ethos.	• Parents could be sure that the school was trying to encourage traditional academic standards.
• Teachers were committed to the rules which they saw as a vital compensatory factor.	• Teachers saw the rules as a reinforcement of the standards of a Catholic upbringing.	• Teachers agreed that good work habits were linked to good discipline.
• The children felt secure in knowing the consistent nature of school expectations.	• Pupils had a clear standard to aim for.	• Pupils understood that school standards were associated with work.
Costs	***Costs***	***Costs***
• Parents did not relate naturally to the rules. They saw them as reflecting school values.	• Possible difficulty for parents who did not fully internalise the Catholic ethos.	• Some parents might find difficulty in identifying with the traditional academic curriculum.
• Pupils had to balance two different sets of standards – home and school.	• Pupils could take a 'black and white' view of school standards.	• Some pupils might find difficulty in identifying with the traditional academic curriculum.
• Teachers might stress good behaviour at the expense of good work.		• Teachers may find that they are equating 'good work' with 'good behaviour'.
	Benefits	
	• Parents could feel they understood and agreed with school objectives for their children.	
	• Teachers did not have to discuss and apply an alternative set of standards.	
	• Pupils understood that school standards and home standards were similar.	
	Costs	
	• Some parents might require a more explicit definition of the school rules.	
	• Some pupils might require a more explicit definition of the school rules.	
	• Successful application of the rules was dependent upon the individual teacher's skill and experience.	

is that there is no one right way to involve parents and Table 7.1 tries to explore the possible benefits and costs of the approaches adopted in our four schools.

Assessing parental involvement in your school

What kind of message do you give to parents? What kind of message do you want to give? We suggest that you attempt to look objectively at the ways in which your school contacts parents; for example:

- Read over the school brochure as if you were a parent. What kind of expectations does your school have? What kind of language do you use?
- How are parents encouraged to contact the school?
- Who deals with parents? Can they see the class teacher directly?
- Where do you take your general knowledge of parents from? Local housing? The pupils' stories? Local gossip? Day-to-day observation? How accurate is this, do you think?

Many schools pay lip service to the idea of parental involvement. This is understandable; the school has standards to keep up and professional demands which cannot be altered for every individual pupil. Nevertheless, if parental involvement is to be more than a good idea, teachers will have to find out more about who the parents really are. Consider using governors as a way of enhancing home–school communication and of involving parents more directly in school life.

References

Bastiani, J. (ed.) (1988) *Parents and Teachers 2: From Policy to Practice*, NFER-Nelson, London.

Craft, M., Rayner, J. and Cohen, L. (eds.) (1980) *Linking Home and School*, Harper & Row, London.

Cullingford, C. (1985) *Parents, Teachers and Schools*, Royce, London.

Douglas, J., Ross, J. and Simpson, H. R. (1968) *All Our Future: A Longitudinal Study of Secondary Education*, Peter Davies, London.

Fraser, E. (1959) *Home Environment and the School*, University Press, London.

Hargreaves, D., Hestor, S. and Mellor, F. (1975) *Deviance in Classrooms*, Routledge & Kegan Paul, London.

Hewison, J. (1985) The evidence of case studies of parents' involvement in schools, in C. Cullingford (ed.) op. cit.

Jackson, A. and Hannon, P. (1981) *The Belfield Reading Project*, Belfield Community Council, Rochdale.

Johnson, D. and Ransom, E. (1983) *Family and School*, Croom Helm, Beckenham.

Lawrence, J., Steed, D. and Young, P. (1984) *Disruptive Children – Disruptive Schools?*, Croom Helm, Beckenham.

Macbeth, A. (1989) *Involving Parents: Effective Parent–Teacher Relations*, Heinemann Organisation in Schools Series, London.

Marjoribanks, R. (1979) *Families and their Learning Environments: An Empirical Analysis*, Routledge & Kegan Paul, London.

Mays, J. (1980) The impact of neighbourhood values, in Craft *et al.*, op. cit.

Meighan, R. (1981) A new teaching force? Some issues raised by seeing parents as educators and the implications for teacher education, *Educational Review*, 33, 2, pp. 133–142.

Prosser, M. (1981) The myth of parental apathy, *Times Educational Supplement*, 16.10.81, pp. 22–23.

Sharp, R. and Green, A. (1975) *Education and Social Control: A Study in Progressive Primary Education*, Routledge & Kegan Paul, London.

Tattum, D. (1982) *Disruptive Children in Schools and Units*, Wiley, Chichester.

Tizard, B. (1987) Parent involvement – a no-score draw? *Times Educational Supplement*, 3.4.87.

Tizard, B. and Hughes, M. (1984) *Young Children Learning: Talking and Thinking at Home and in School*, Fontana, London.

Wheldall, K. and Merrett, F. (1988) Which classroom behaviours do primary school teachers say they find troublesome? *Educational Review*, 40, 1, pp. 13–28.

8
WHAT CAN SCHOOLS DO TO IMPROVE DISCIPLINE?

We began this book by stressing that there is no magic recipe for effective discipline. What works and is seen as effective in one school will not necessarily work in another. Each school has its own particular circumstances to take into account. However, we believe that our research has indicated some key areas which schools could begin to address if they want to improve discipline. These areas are:

- the school's expectations about its pupils;
- staff relationships and the special role of the headteacher;
- the extent and quality of parental involvement.

Although we have devoted a chapter to each of these aspects, they are all closely connected. We have separated them only to clarify them as components of that hard-to-measure phenomenon, school ethos.

We can illustrate the interconnections by reference to one example, that of Westway. Westway expected that many of its pupils would not be aware of some of the values which the school held dear. Values such as the importance of regular attendance, punctuality, courtesy and tolerance, for example, could not be taken for granted as important in the kind of catchment area in which the school was situated. Westway, therefore, had clear rules which staff took considerable trouble to explain to the pupils. In addition, the teachers went to great lengths to explain the rationale for the rules. The sanctions used when rules were broken involved parents on such matters as attendance and punctuality in an attempt to convey school values to the home, but for other offences in-school sanctions were preferred, since the automatic support of parents could not be assumed. In general, contact with parents had been slight, although the new head was changing policy in this area. There was an open sharing of discipline problems among staff and the head was highly visible around the school.

It seemed to us that these interconnections were highly logical, given the staff's views of the catchment area and, crucially, the belief that the school could make a difference, that it was the school's responsibility to convey particular values. If parental support could not be taken for granted, it was logical to assume that pupils might be exposed to different and conflicting home and school values. A way of inculcating school values was through explanation and an appeal to pupils' rationality. The lack of congruence between home and school meant that school values had to be consistently expressed and applied and consistently presented as rational. Conflicting values within the school itself would have further confused the pupils. Therefore, considerable emphasis was put on staff co-operation and on headteacher support. Assumptions about lack of parental support had meant that, in the past, efforts at involving parents more actively in their children's schooling were not a high priority. The new head was changing this, in the belief that parental support could be harnessed, that the school could reach out into the community, and that this would have positive effects. The whole approach had its own inner logic. The system worked in the opinion of staff and HMI had praised the school for its caring approach.

The system worked because of the kind of school Westway was. It would be facile to suppose that the approach could be lifted, lock, stock and barrel and transplanted, for example, into Braidburn. Schools do not operate in a vacuum. As we have indicated above, their history, including for example, the kinds of pupils who attend, the level of staff turnover, their physical location and the expectations held by parents, influences school discipline. The expectations which a school has of its pupils or, more generally, how it develops its ethos, is not a matter of unfettered choice by the teachers.

School discipline, then, operates in a context where room for manoeuvre is limited and bringing about change is a subtle and complicated matter, involving teachers, parents and pupils. Indeed, the management of change has provoked an extensive literature with much advice about ownership, incentives, action plans and monitoring. This is not to say that change is impossible; far from it. One of the complaints about the current state of schools is that there have been too many changes and that teachers are suffering from 'innovation fatigue'. Bringing about any real and lasting change takes time and as much thought needs to be given to the process as to the substantive area of change itself.

Any school setting about improving its discipline is, therefore, undertaking a major task which goes to the heart of the way the school sees itself. We say this not to put teachers off but to highlight the commitment and enthusiasm needed to bring about change and improvement. Writers stress that there is no point in less effective schools mimicking the more effective by replicating some of their characteristics, such as displaying pupils' work or having homework timetables. These are the surface characteristics of a school's values and emphasis and it is these which lie at the core of real change and improvement. The same point holds for school discipline. The four schools described in this book had their own distinctive approach which reflected their values. We have argued that each approach had benefits and costs, and that what worked in Westway would not work in Braidburn or vice versa. What does this mean for schools wanting to improve their discipline? First, that real improvement will come about only if staff, particularly the headteacher, want it to happen. Second, that improvement means more than cosmetic adjustments to rules, sanctions, rewards and pastoral care systems. These reflect a school's value system. Third, that schools need to make explicit their values and emphasis before they can change them.

The following is a checklist of steps that can be taken to examine what schools take for granted about their approach to discipline. It is quite long and no school would want to pursue all these activities at once. One approach might be for an interested and committed group of staff to choose one area and see what they come up with. Another might be for the group to divide up tasks among themselves with one sub-group investigating the school's expectations of pupils and another examining management roles, for example. The important point is that once the school begins to investigate its own practice it can see the extent of match and mismatch between intention and reality. It can then begin to develop ways of minimising any mismatch, perhaps by using the case studies in this book as a stimulus for discussion and debate, and coming up with its own solutions.

A checklist for examining school discipline

Expectations of pupils

- Read the school brochure as if you were a stranger. What expectations of pupils does it convey? Are these the ones you intend? If not, how do you bring about more than a cosmetic change in the text?
- Look at the school rules. Are the published rules seen as the really important ones? Do they signal expectations of bad behaviour by emphasising don'ts rather than dos?
- What messages are conveyed by the sanctions used for rule breakers?
- Does the school have any rewards for good behaviour or is the emphasis on bad behaviour being punished?
- Find out what pupils think. Ask a group to write about school rules, rewards and punishments.

Expectations of teachers

- How much freedom do teachers have to set their own standards of behaviour? Find out by asking some teachers and pupils: do not assume you know. Should there be more or less freedom? Why?
- Find out what new staff, probationers and students know about the school's discipline policy. Are they clear about rules, rewards, sanctions, referral systems and sources of support? Is the staff handbook helpful on discipline? If it needs improving, could new staff help with redrafting?

- Analyse the layout of the school. Are there particular trouble-spots? Who is responsible for supervising these? Are all staff expected to deal with indiscipline anywhere in the school? What are the advantages and disadvantages of this?
- What would you say were the dominant purposes of teaching in the school? How confident are you that your view is shared by most staff? Check up.

Expectations of parents

- Analyse some recent typical communication from school to parents as if you were a stranger. What messages does it convey about the school's attitude to parents? Think about language register, tone, notions of partnership.
- How often do you communicate good news about the school, or about individual children to parents? Analyse the pattern of communication with a group of parents over a term with regard to, for example, year groups, complaints, good news, fund-raising, welcoming involvement in school activities, sharing expectations about behaviour and asking for support before problems arise.
- Could parents be more actively involved in shaping and maintaining school discipline? If so, think about ways of involving the PTA and/or governors as a starting point.

Expectations about senior management: practical activities for senior staff

- Keep a diary of your own involvement in discipline over a week. What image does it convey? Is this the image you intend?
- Ask one or two staff to keep a diary for a week about their involvement in discipline. What do these and your own diaries tell you about communication channels, feedback to staff, pupils and parents, and the extent of involvement of different staff in discipline matters?
- Find out what staff and pupils think about the role senior management plays in discipline. You could develop a short and simple questionnaire about this.

As we stressed in introducing this checklist, no school could undertake all of these activities at once. These activities are suggestions, ways of getting started. Some involve desk activities, such as analysing the school brochure or the school's communication with parents over a term. Others require active data-gathering from teachers and pupils. The important thing is that they offer ways of challenging assumptions about the way discipline works in your school. Some of your assumptions will be well founded; others less so. When surprises and/or disappointments about the effectiveness of discipline are revealed, this in turn provides a basis for developing and improving policy. It seems to us that such an approach stands a better chance of sustained and real improvement in discipline than trying 'one damn thing after another'.

We have deliberately omitted from the checklist questions concerning the adequacy of the school curriculum. Previous research has shown what a dominant influence on pupil behaviour this can be. Primary schools now have to implement the National Curriculum and assess pupils' progress and attainment in accordance with pre-specified targets and levels. Changes in curriculum and assessment *may* have a positive spin-off in terms of pupils' behaviour, although there is no clear national evidence yet that this is so. In any event, schools are in the throes of large-scale curriculum change and are already devoting energy to this area.

Our questions are drawn directly from our data and are designed to help teachers and headteachers examine what they necessarily have to take for granted in the day-to-day running of the school. We cannot suggest that there are right answers to these questions. We can suggest that, whatever the answer, there are benefits and costs and we have illustrated these for the case-study schools. Staff in other schools might see things differently; much depends on the school context. We hope, however, that our analysis of benefits and costs of the various views schools held of their pupils, of the relationships among staff and about parental involvement, help staff to look critically at their own school if they are concerned about reviewing discipline policy and practice. Fundamentally, of course, we have no research evidence from this study on how a school might set about making changes. Our concern has been with describing what we have called key ideas about the influences on whole school discipline. How to bring about change in schools has been the subject of a good deal of research and the literature has been reviewed elsewhere. Perhaps the main point to make is the need to convince all those involved in the change that it is worthwhile for them, that school life will, in some sense, be better as a result.

Three other points are worth making before leaving whole school discipline. The first concerns the role of the education authority. For most of the teachers in the case studies, the authority was a remote, distant entity. The authorities would, in fact, have had official policies on various aspects of school life, which were not necessarily obvious to school staff. Teachers seemed to have very little contact with regional education officers, and this is not surprising. Local authority officers are few in number and it would be difficult for them to make contact with teaching staff as a matter of routine. They were available in times of trouble, such as when decisions to exclude pupils were in the offing, but data about the influence of the region on school discipline were conspicuous by their absence. This is hardly surprising. It is teachers who have day-to-day responsibilities for discipline and, of necessity, they are concerned with the particular, rather than the strategic.

The second point is more difficult to relate straightforwardly to school discipline. This is the change which seems to have occurred in teachers' views of their responsibilities following the dispute in 1983 in Scotland. Staff in all our schools referred to this dispute and most saw it as deeply damaging. The move towards a contract specifying responsibilities has, in most of the schools we researched, led to a reduction of responsibilities teachers are willing to accept. In some of the schools this was manifested by a radical reduction in extra-curricular activities, which in the past had helped to develop pupil–teacher relationships. In other schools, although extra-curricular work had picked up again, teachers were much less willing to see themselves as responsible for discipline in school corridors and playgrounds. We have no wish to enter into a history of the dispute. We wish merely to point out that its effects were mentioned to us in all our schools and these were seen as detrimental to discipline. Clearly, any feelings of being undervalued, or not being trusted to get on with the job, will affect teachers' enthusiasm and willingness to examine school policy on discipline or on anything else.

The third and most important point is that these typical schools were pleasant and purposeful environments in which to undertake research. As indicated at the outset, we had no independent measures of effective discipline but relied on teachers' and pupils' views of effectiveness. However, we think it is important to make clear that the schools were not hot-beds of disruption and disaffection. Participation in the life of these schools over a few weeks suggested considerable congruence between what staff and pupils told us and what we saw. So that when, for example, teachers told us that they shared problems, or that the head was highly visible around the school, we witnessed these things in operation. From the perspective of detached observers, the schools were happy and productive places for teachers and pupils.

Classroom discipline

Our study of the ways in which eight experienced teachers got their classes to work well revealed strong similarities among them. This was despite the fact that they worked in different schools and taught different age groups of pupils. The things which these teachers had in common were:

- their emphasis on preparation and planning. Over half their actions concerned setting the framework for a lesson. This reinforces the point, made by many other studies, that experienced teachers plan to avoid the occurrence of disruption by making sure that pupils know what they have to do and that the relevant materials are to hand, and have inculcated routines concerning, for example, movement around the room, the beginning and ending of lessons and the use of equipment.
- their constant monitoring of pupil activity and dealing with minor disruption. Good discipline is not something which is established once and for all. It has to be constantly worked at, reinforcing rules and routines when the situation demands it.
- the importance of their knowledge of individual pupils and of the class as a whole in influencing the actions taken.
- their clear image of what a normal desirable state of pupils' activity should be in any curriculum task. Each worked towards establishing this normal desirable state.

Chapters 4 and 5 deal with teachers' actions and then with influences on those actions in detail. However, there are many excellent texts already in existence which offer help and advice to teachers on classroom discipline. Is our work offering anything new? Our answer would be 'yes', because, for the first time, teachers' classroom actions are embedded in a conceptual framework which describes and explains the interconnections between these actions and what we have called goals and conditions – a framework derived from teachers' own comments about what they do and why they do it, rather than abstract intellectualising about what teachers ought to be doing. It is this framework which we hope will be of most use to those concerned with classroom practice because it provides one way of making sense of teaching. So often beginning teachers observe experienced teachers in action, noting the smooth transitions from one activity to another and the organisation of groups of children engaged on different tasks, only to find that, when they take the place of the experienced teacher, classroom organisation comes apart at the seams. Part of the explanation for this state of affairs is that beginning teachers are not skilled observers of classrooms. They do not know what they are supposed to be looking for, nor are they able to discern influences on what the teacher is doing. The great temptation is to become a member of the class, albeit an adult member, following the course of activities rather than thinking about what the teacher is doing and why. Our framework could help new teachers to:

- observe experienced teachers more systematically;
- reflect on their own practice;
- develop their lesson planning by making them think explicitly about their goals, and the conditions influencing their goals and actions.

Of course, we would not wish to claim too much for our framework. We are confident that we have gained access to some of teachers' craft knowledge about promoting and maintaining discipline. Our confidence rests on the consistency of the accounts the teachers presented. Teachers from different schools, teaching pupils of different ages and who had diverse initial training, talked in similar ways. They have also endorsed our interpretation of the ways in which they talked when we fed back our analysis to them. Another reason for our confidence is in the face validity of our framework. It seems to make sense to other teachers who find it easy to identify with. However, we are sure that we have not fully mapped teachers' professional craft knowledge about discipline. By concentrating on what teachers do to get their classes to work well, we have underrepresented how they deal with discipline problems. Nevertheless, we hope we have provided a useful starting point for thinking about what experienced teachers do routinely and spontaneously in their classrooms.

Links between whole school and classroom practice

There have been two main strands to our work on discipline: whole school policy and practice, and classroom practice.

At the whole school level we have shown that there are key ideas which underpin whole school policy and which influence the way in which that policy works in practice. At classroom level we have produced a conceptual framework for understanding classroom discipline and a list of actions, goals and conditions which influence classroom discipline. We have seen our whole school work as having implications for school development plans by providing a starting point for whole school review and our classroom work as having implications for pre-service training. It is tempting but mistaken to see these two strands as separate. We want to conclude by emphasising the links between them. The main link, in our opinion, is the expectations of pupils which schools hold. These expectations are a major influence on the goals which teachers set for their pupils and so on what counts as effective discipline in their classrooms. In Chapter 5 we showed that one of the most important influences on the actions teachers took to maintain discipline was knowledge of the pupils. Expectations about pupils seemed to us to be strongly influenced by the catchment area of the school. Of course, this was not the only influence. Teachers had beliefs about the nature and purpose of teaching, for example, and, as already stated, the history of the school was important. However, our research suggests the fundamental importance of expectations about pupils for both whole school and classroom discipline and we have summarised the connections in Figure 8.1.

Table 8.1: Links between whole school and classroom discipline

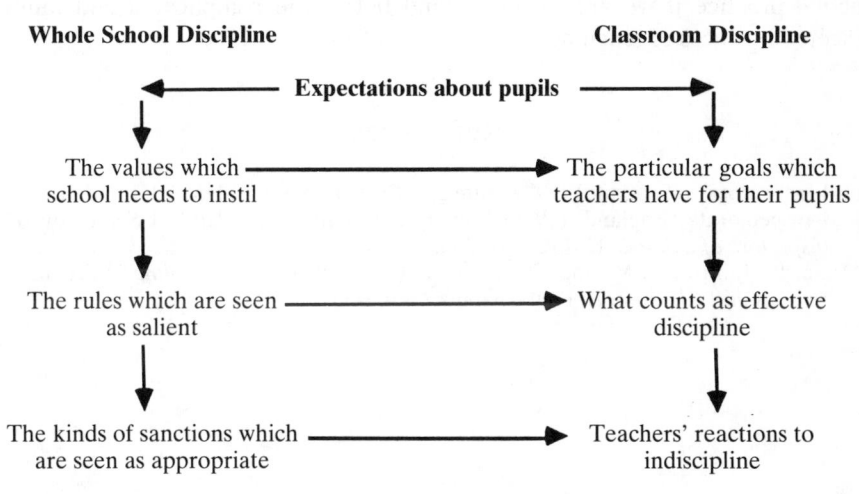

We recognise that this is only part of the story. Of course, the role of the headteacher and senior staff, relationships among staff and attitudes towards involving parents are a few of the many influences on discipline, to say nothing of national initiatives on curriculum and assessment, quality assurance and teacher appraisal. Similarly, a whole host of influences impinge on classroom teaching. Our simple purpose in emphasising the explicit connections between whole school and classroom practice is to stress that school managers (headteachers and other senior staff) need to be very much aware of how school policy is operationalised in classrooms. Similarly, teachers' classroom practice has direct repercussions on whole school policy.

As in all research, we are left wanting to know more. The further exploration of teachers' professional craft knowledge seems to us to be a fruitful way forward in extending knowledge about teaching. Questions which seem worthy of further research are:

- How do teachers establish effective routines?
- How do teachers build up repertoires of actions to use in particular circumstances?
- Does subject-specific knowledge, for example in environmental studies or number, influence pedagogy? If so, in what ways?

Such research would be useful not only in extending knowledge for its own sake, but to contribute to our understanding of implementing innovations. Unless we know more about the nature of teaching we cannot predict whether innovations are congruent with teachers' classroom practice or so antithetical that they stand little chance of being adopted. Similarly, we can appraise teaching only if we understand better what it is. Finally, we can improve teacher education only if we know more about the teachers' craft. Such knowledge needs to be elicited from experienced teachers and grounded in actual practice if we are to understand better the complicated and multi-faceted business of teaching.

References

HM Inspectorate (Scotland) (1989) *Effective Primary Schools*, HMSO, London.
HM Inspectorate (England) (1978) *Primary Education in England: A Survey by HM Inspectors of Schools*, HMSO, London.
Munn, P., Johnstone, M. and Chalmers, V. (1992) *Effective Discipline in Secondary Schools and Classrooms*, Paul Chapman, London.

RESEARCH APPENDIX: RESEARCH DESIGN, DATA COLLECTION AND ANALYSIS

This appendix sets out in greater detail than was possible in the main text:

- the rationale for a case-study approach;
- the methods used to collect and analyse data on whole school discipline;
- the methods used to collect and analyse data on classroom discipline.

Before describing these details it is important to make clear that the research was commissioned by the Scottish Office Education Department (SOED) as part of its policy-related research programme. The research questions were largely pre-specified although our proposal focused particularly on whole school and on classroom discipline to the exclusion of other matters of interest to the SOED such as the role of the regional authority in school discipline and the role of parents. Our justification for this was that whole school and classroom discipline were areas which teachers could do something about, were they so minded. These were areas which were more directly under teachers' influence than, for example, parental attitudes towards behaviour or social mores. Similarly, since the purpose of the research was to understand effective discipline, a study of deviant pupil behaviour or liaison between schools and the psychological or social services was seen by us as inappropriate. The main research questions are given on pages 4–5. It may be useful to remind ourselves that they concerned:

- what counted as effective discipline;
- the support available to promote effective discipline and to deal with indiscipline;
- whether indiscipline was defined and measured;
- the criteria used by pupils to describe how their teachers got the class 'to work well';
- how 'effective disciplinarians' operated in their classrooms.

The methods used to address these areas at a whole school level differed from those used in the classroom research. Before describing these, however, we say a brief word about the rationale for a case-study approach.

The rationale for a case-study approach

Our own (Johnstone and Munn, 1987) and other reviews of the literature on discipline (e.g. Docking, 1987) reveal the many different research approaches used to investigate the topic. These range from large-scale surveys focusing on particular kinds of indiscipline, such as truancy, to case-studies of schools, classrooms and special units. Clearly, all approaches have their strengths and weaknesses depending on the research questions being addressed and the hoped-for outcomes of the work.

Our starting point was that we wanted to understand why schools and teachers adopted their particular approaches to promoting and maintaining discipline. We knew that contextual factors were important in defining and promoting discipline but we had no clear hypothesis about which factors were important or about how factors operated. This ruled out a large-scale survey. A survey in such circumstances would have provided us with descriptive information about the policy and practice of large numbers of schools and teachers but it would have little explanatory power. Indeed, a survey could provide a useful general backdrop to more detailed work and provide answers to questions about the salience of discipline as an issue for teachers. It could not extend our knowledge of why schools and teachers promoted and maintained discipline in particular ways.

Case-study work, it seemed to us, offered the possibility of uncovering explanations for schools' and teachers' actions. The case studies were at two levels, that of whole school (four schools were studied in depth) and of individual teachers (the classroom practice of eight teachers was researched). The possibility of explanation was provided by semi-structured interviewing about whole school policy and practice and open-ended interviewing about classroom practice. Case-study also meant we could spend a considerable period of time in each school and get to know the staff, the rhythms of school life and observe at first hand the discipline systems in operation.

Clearly, the experience of four schools is not generalisable in a statistical sense. Our identification of key ideas influencing whole school discipline and of a conceptual framework for understanding classroom discipline can be tested by schools and teachers interested in understanding their own practice. We see ourselves as providing conceptual and analytic tools for thinking about whole school and classroom discipline. We do not see ourselves as providing solutions for schools and teachers who want to solve problems of indiscipline, except insofar as we provide them with a place to start in understanding their practice and the areas to attend to in developing policy and practice.

Whole school discipline

Data collection and analysis : from teachers

A pilot study (Johnstone and Munn, 1987b) had enabled us to explore the feasibility of semi-structured interviewing about whole school discipline. It also alerted us to the need to sample a range of subject departments in the secondary school. In the primary school, our object was to interview one teacher at each of the stages P1 to P7 inclusive, to gain an overall picture of the school. In addition, the headteacher, the depute head and/or assistant headteacher were also interviewed. Where feasible, we also interviewed other staff, for example, the learning support teacher or nursery staff. Table 1 gives details of the teachers interviewed.

Table 1: Numbers of staff interviewed

Headteacher	AHT (EE)	Depute	*Teachers	†Others	Total
4	4	1	32	4	45

*In one school, both P6 teachers were interviewed to give 100% representation of the staff; in another school, three teachers of composite classes were interviewed for the same reason.
†Includes learning support teacher, auxiliary teacher and supply teacher.

The teachers were interviewed using a semi-structured schedule which covered the main areas of the research questions. There was a set introduction and ending but beyond this the interviewer tried to be responsive to matters raised by the interviewees and to use these matters to move from one area to another or to probe for more detail. All the interviews were tape-recorded and conducted in private. They lasted between forty-five minutes and an hour.

All the interviews were transcribed and a coding frame built up from the research questions. The frame was initially derived from a sample of interviews analysed independently by the three members of the research team. It was extended slightly on a subsequent sample and the initial sample was re-analysed using the new frame. Some data fell outside the coding frame. These initially were coded separately and some became 'core ideas' because of their recurrence and prominence in the transcripts.

Data collection and analysis: from pupils

The same sample of pupils was used for whole school and classroom data. A total of 301 pupils, that is all P6 and P7 pupils in the four schools, were asked to complete a series of open-ended booklets. These three booklets had been piloted with primary school children in a different region; the results indicated that P5 pupils had found some difficulties in understanding the task, but that

P6 and P7 pupils were, in the main, capable of a clear response. Each of the separate booklets covered a different aspect of discipline:

- what your teacher does to get the class to work well;
- what are the classroom rules and what happens when they are broken?
- what are the school rules and what happens when they are broken?

In all four of the case-study schools the three booklets were given to the pupils in sequence, in their own classrooms. In each case the administration of the booklets was carried out by a researcher, not the class teacher.

The pupils found it relatively straightforward to write about what their teacher did. Descriptions of the classroom sanctions used when rules were broken were also clear, but it was more difficult for pupils to write about school rules and sanctions. A percentage of the pupils noted that, in fact, they didn't always know what happened to someone who broke a school rule (see Chapter 6 for details of the pupil response).

The rules data were analysed according to a coding frame established from a sample of scripts and independently checked. Each school's pupil sample was analysed as a unit. In this way we were able to establish a rank order for the most salient rules for pupils in each school. This served as illustration for some of the key ideas emerging more generally from the research.

We attempted to obtain some picture of the views of the younger pupils by interviewing them in small groups. Our initial plan was to interview pupils from the infants and from the middle school, using a semi-structured schedule and recording the interviews. In one school we were discouraged from recording pupils; the headteacher felt that this would entail too much explanation to parents. In all of the schools, 'interviewing' infants proved an elusive if instructive task. The end result was a series of group interviews of different quality, different range and different context. These were used purely as illustrative material (see Chapter 6).

Data collection and analysis: from documents

The ways in which a school presents its policy in print was an aspect which we felt had some relevance to the research study. Each of the schools had provided us with a copy of its brochure or prospectus. We examined the format and content of these documents to find out whether there were differences in the ways these schools set out their aims for pupils. We looked at the extent to which schools emphasised one approach to discipline as opposed to another. We also looked at the school's policy on the involvement of parents in the community. Where there were policy papers in the school we also examined those but, on the whole, the primary schools seemed less paperbound than the secondary schools. This analysis of the school documentation illuminated the key ideas, as the main text shows.

Data collection and analysis: from field notes

Each researcher completed a descriptive profile of her specific schools; that is, number of teachers, classes, pupils, placement requests, and the pattern of specialist teaching, learning support, nursery provision and provision of support from the educational psychologist. Beyond this, each researcher kept a daily diary for each school visit. This gave details of the current fabric of the school, the presence or absence of parents, the visits of 'outside' people, the concerns of the janitor, the auxiliaries and the school secretary, and reports of the incidents of the day. These field notes may not have covered everything that happened during the researcher's time in the school, but they did provide substantial supportive and illustrative data. This data underpins Chapters 2 and 3 specifically.

Classroom discipline

There were two main approaches to collecting information about what teachers did in their classrooms to get the class to work well. We observed teachers with their classes and we talked to them about what they did. These interviews were focused on a particular teaching segment of the school day, during which the observer had been present in the classroom.

We observed each of the eight teachers for part of a day, over a total per teacher of between seven and twelve days (see Chapter 4 for an explanation of the selection of the teachers). Some of the teachers preferred a longer observation period than others; all of them discussed their plans with the researcher(s) so that a variety of observations of different subject areas and teaching approaches was possible. The classes involved ranged in stage from P1 through to P7, and included two composite classes. Only P4 was not represented. Observing two teachers in each school over a period of weeks gave both teachers and pupils time to get used to our presence. Although we would not claim to have been invisible to the pupils, it did seem that even the infants were able to discount or forget our presence for most of the observation time.

The observation itself was non-participant and relatively unstructured. We took no part in the teaching and tried to avoid giving auxiliary help in the infants' classrooms (e.g. tying shoelaces). For each observation period we noted in general terms what the teacher and pupils were doing (Walker and Adelman, 1987). We used a time frame of two-minute intervals. Particular care was taken to note the teacher's movements around the room, and any non-verbal cues used. The main purpose of these notes was simply to provide a record as a shared reference point for the teacher and researcher to discuss. A tape-recording of the lesson might have been more objective, although such a recording would necessarily have to be complemented by a note of non-verbal behaviours. We had, in fact, used radio microphone recordings of lessons with the secondary school teachers, but these recordings were never used as a reminder to teachers of the flow of the lesson. The secondary school teachers either did not need any reminding of the lesson, or they were happy to use the researcher's notes as a prompt. The potential disruption of setting up a radio recording did not seem to be compensated for by clearer or more detailed interviews.

As near as possible to the observed lesson, sometimes directly afterwards, usually in the nearest break or lunchtime, we asked the teacher, 'What did you do to get the class to work well?' The teachers found this a very difficult question to answer. We were asking them to make explicit their routine, taken-for-granted behaviour in their classrooms. We had many requests from the teachers to suggest what *we* thought they had done to get the class to work well, but the whole point of our approach was to elicit from teachers their own constructs of what they did. This meant that initial interviews were often very brief, perhaps five minutes or so, as teachers said all they had to say about their practice. Our only probes were, 'Can you tell me a bit more about that?' and 'Why did you do that?' and 'Was that the same as in lesson such and such?' However, as time went on, the teachers gradually had more to say, perhaps because they knew they were going to be talking about their actions and so became more conscious of them. It may be, of course, that they became more expert at providing 'rationalisations' rather than 'true explanations' of their practice. Our approach to collecting and analysing the information about teachers' classroom practice closely mirrors that of Brown and McIntyre (1989) in their study of teachers' professional craft knowledge and we say more about our analysis of the data below.

Data analysis

In analysing the data we tried to follow the same procedure as that adopted by Brown and McIntyre (1989). This involved the following sequence:

- analysing (independently) a pair of teachers' interview transcripts;
- identifying their actions for promoting and maintaining discipline at a descriptive level;
- generating concepts which helped illuminate the teachers' comments about actions;
- re-analysing the transcripts using the concepts;
- identifying the data not covered by the concepts;
- moving on to the next teachers' transcripts and using the concepts;
- identifying their actions for promoting and maintaining discipline;
- trying out the concepts previously generated, and so on.

This procedure was used for all transcripts. As can be imagined, it was a time-consuming process but one which would, we hoped, generate hypotheses to be carried from one teacher interview to the next. There was a good deal of brainstorming, of bouncing ideas off one another and it was very important to have at least three of us involved in the work so that concepts could be debated and rejected, or affirmed. The generalisations which we were able to establish as a result of this process were seen as providing the basis for the theoretical framework in Chapter 4. However, in generating this theoretical framework we are, again, indebted to Brown and McIntyre (1989) for their identification of the criteria which had to be met in order for the theoretical framework to count as grounded in the data. These criteria were as follows:

- all aspects of the framework had to be directly supported by evidence (it is easy to add key elements which create a coherent abstract system but are not themselves observable in the data);
- the generalisations had to relate to normal practice, not to what the teacher did on rare occasions;
- where the generalisations went beyond one person and one occasion, they had to be based on data for each teacher and from each of that teacher's lessons;
- it was not sufficient to identify a series of generalisable but isolated elements as what teachers know or think; the relationships between these elements had to be identified;
- the framework should not discount any part of the teacher's account as 'diverging from relevant matters';
- the theoretical account of the teacher's knowledge and thinking had to be accepted by the teacher as a balanced and adequate account.

These demanding criteria were difficult to meet in full. For example, some data were excluded from our analysis because the interviewer had led the respondents, from time to time, by suggesting to them particular actions for maintaining discipline. Sometimes teachers talked about their ideal behaviour rather than their actual behaviour and these data were discounted, too, although we have made use of them, outside the generation of a conceptual framework, to speculate about how teachers come to acquire their routines and repertoires of actions.

When we had constructed the conceptual framework, we fed this back to the eight teachers, with a brief explanatory paper. Each element of the framework was illustrated by quotations from that teacher. None of the teachers felt that the framework misrepresented what they had said, although in one case there was a slight semantic confusion. This endorsement, together with the consistency of the accounts presented by these teachers from four different schools, teaching pupils at different stages and with different pre-service training, gave us confidence that the framework accessed a part of teachers' craft knowledge. We should add that the conceptual framework has been discussed with several different teacher groups, who have found it easy to identify with, and who feel that it makes sense. We find a degree of face validity in this reaction.

Conclusion

We have attempted to describe the measures used in the research, the samples selected and the methods of data analysis used. Perhaps we should stress the value of piloting in relation to our successful paper-and-pencil measure with pupils; this was time-consuming but very effective in clearing the ground. The piloting of appropriate ways to carry out case-study research was highly valuable.

We hope that this appendix answers the questions which occur to fellow researchers reading the main text. These readers will recognise that this appendix could have been twice as long if justice were done to the consultations, discussions, refinements and decisions made during the three years of the research. Examples of interview schedules and the instruments used to collect data from pupils are available directly from SCRE on request.

References

Brown, S. and McIntyre, D. (1989) *Making Sense of Teaching*, Scottish Council for Research in Education, Edinburgh.

Docking, J. (1987) *Control and Discipline in Schools: Perspectives and Approaches Second Edition*, Paul Chapman, London.

Johnstone, M. and Munn, P. (1987a) *Discipline in School: A review of 'causes' and 'cures'*, Scottish Council for Research in Education, Edinburgh.

Johnstone, M. and Munn, P. (1987b) *Discipline: A pilot study*, Scottish Council for Research in Education, Edinburgh.

Walker, R. and Adelman, C. (1987) *A Guide to Classroom Observation*, Methuen, London.

SUBJECT INDEX

absence 23, 27

assistant headteacher 7, 8, 9, 10, 45–6

autonomy: parental impact on 107, 109, 110; professional freedom 23, 48, 54; restrictions on 47

beginning teachers 12, 44, 69–72, 82, 88, 128

Braidburn School 9, 14, 21–2

catchment area: description of 7, 8, 9, 10; relevance to pupil behaviour 30, 32, 109, 111

Catholic education 52, 115

classroom context (conditions): range of 62–4, 79–83; and actions 86–7

classroom discipline: influences on (*see also* goals and classroom context) 62–5; proactive approaches 60–1, 75, 127; teachers' reactions to disruption 62, 75, 127

class size 82

curriculum 107, 125–6

discipline: definitions of 2–3; school definitions 110, 111, 114, 116; pupils' views 102, 112

discipline policy 45, 105–6

early education/infants 43–4, 47, 51, 60, 111

education authorities 6–7, 126

exclusion 28, 35

extra curricular activities 109, 110, 117

frameworks: linking school and classroom 128–9; for understanding classroom discipline 59, 66–8, 69, 81, 127–8

goals for pupils: avoidance 85; influences on classroom discipline 64–5, 66–8, 86–7; normal desirable state 83–5, 86; progress 85, 84–5, 86; punishment 85, 86; reward 85, 86

headteacher: contact with parents 112–3, 116; role of 41, 42–5, 47–8; and teaching 41, 44; visibility of 48, 54, 122

HM Inspectorate of Schools 29, 123

industrial dispute 10, 114, 116, 126–7

labelling 17, 24

legislation 104–5, 107, 115

Oldtown School 10, 14, 22–23

parent/parent-teacher association: existence of 9, 10; and discipline 108, 109, 112, 114, 116

parents: school relationship with 21; and school discipline policy 106–8 (*see also* relationships and sanctions)

punishment exercises 30–1, 97, 98

pupils: assumptions made by schools 18–23; home background of 18–9, 20, 21–4; 'ownership of' 49–51; with learning difficulties 107

rebukes 25, 28–9, 75, 90, 92

relationships: management-teacher 30, 42, 47; parent-teacher 108–117; pupil-teacher 24–6, 29, 32, 95; teacher-teacher 42, 51–52

research approach: aims 4–5; claims 11–3; methods 11, 18, 58–9, 74–5, 89–90

rewards: points system 32; rewarding
teachers 50; use of praise 31–2, 78
rules: in each school 19–20, 23;
comparison among schools 26–8, 122;
pupils' views 33, 34, 78, 95, 98, 100–2

St Veronica's School 8–9, 14, 18–20
Sanctions: in each school 21, 25, 28;
pupils' views 43, 90, 92, 94, 97, 98,
99–100; used in classrooms 75–8, 98–9;
and parents 104, 108, 114, 122
school board 108, 115
school brochure 18, 21, 23, 105–6
school ethos 54, 122 (*see also* values)

school effectiveness 6, 17–8
school goals 19–20, 21, 23, 29, 33, 35
stress 51
suspension 28, 35

teachers: beliefs about pupils 19, 22, 23,
52; as seen by pupils 90–5 (*see also*
relationships)

values: home-school agreement 109, 114,
home-school conflict 111–2, 117, 123;
school values 34, 122, 123, 124

Westway School 7–8, 14, 18, 20–1